The Witch's Complete Guide to Astrology

chartwell
books

Inspiring | Educating | Creating | Entertaining

Brimming with creative inspiration, how-to projects, and useful information to enrich your everyday life, quarto.com is a favorite destination for those pursuing their interests and passions.

This edition published in 2022 by Chartwell Books,
an imprint of The Quarto Group
142 West 36th Street, 4th Floor
New York, NY 10018 USA

T (212) 779-4972 F (212) 779-6058
www.Quarto.com

10 9 8 7 6 5 4 3 2 1

Chartwell titles are also available at discount for retail, wholesale, promotional, and bulk purchase. For details, contact the Special Sales Manager by email at specialsales@quarto.com or by mail at The Quarto Group, Attn: Special Sales Manager, 100 Cummings Center Suite 265D, Beverly, MA 01915, USA.

ISBN: 978-0-7858-4080-0

Library of Congress Control Number: 2022931179

Publisher: Wendy Friedman
Editorial Director: Betina Cochran
Senior Design Manager: Michael Caputo
Editor: Jennifer Kushnier
Designer: Erin Fahringer

Image credits: Shutterstock

Printed in China

THE WITCH'S COMPLETE GUIDE TO ASTROLOGY

Harness the Heavens and Unlock
Your Potential for a Magical Year

Elsie Wild

chartwell
books

CONTENTS

AN INTRODUCTION TO THE
MAGIC OF THE COSMOS 5

CHAPTER 1: GETTING STARTED 7
* Your Birth Chart and You 7
* Your Big Three................8
* Cleansing Your Space and
  Charging Your Tools 10
* Casting a Protective Circle 11

CHAPTER 2: ZODIAC MAGIC...........12
* Aries 13
* Taurus................21
* Gemini.................29
* Cancer.................37
* Leo.................45
* Virgo.................53
* Libra.................61
* Scorpio.................69
* Sagittarius.................77
* Capricorn.................85
* Aquarius.................93
* Pisces.................99

CHAPTER 3: UNDERSTANDING THE
MAGIC OF THE MOON 106
* The Triple Moon Goddess 107
* The Lunar Phases.................109
* The Moon Through the Signs..........111

CHAPTER 4: THE PLANETS:
THE GUIDING FORCES OF YOUR LIFE
.................128
* Retrogrades 129
* The Sun.................130
* Mercury.................136
* Venus.................142
* Mars.................148
* Jupiter.................154
* Saturn.................156

CHAPTER 5: THE HOUSES 158
* The Houses and Witchcraft...........160

YOUR COSMIC JOURNEY.................167

FURTHER READING AND
RESOURCES 168

An Introduction To The Magic of The Cosmos

Nature plays an important role in our lives, from the grass below our feet to the stars hanging above our heads. But those stars, planets, and even the moon can help shape our destinies as we navigate our way in the world.

That is the magic of astrology.

Astrology is the study of the positions of the stars, planets, and other heavenly bodies and their influence on the natural world. People have been studying the cosmos for centuries, originating in ancient Babylon in 300 BC. While originally used to predict the weather and harvesting cycle, astrology expanded, developed, and spread throughout the world as humans tried to find meaning within the stars.

Today, astrology is used to help predict future events, but it can also be used to learn more about the self and how to unlock the magic within.

No matter what your connection to Wicca is or your level of practice, astrology can help you develop a new and deep connection with your craft and inner magic—whether it's fully embracing the Wheel of the Year, understanding the true magic of the changing seasons, or just learning how important the moon is. It's the stars that guide our craft, and learning the language of the cosmos can help you tap into a new understanding of your spiritual journey.

Astrology and witchcraft are not mutually exclusive. Not all witches use astrology in their craft, just like not all astrologers identify as witches or practice Wicca. However, astrology and Wicca do overlap. Both pay special attention to the moon and its influence on Earth, both use a wheel to help separate seasons and honor the changes of those seasons, and both understand the importance that timing has on our lives. By learning the language of the cosmos, we can find the best ways to boost the power of the planets for our own craft, as well as the best way to unlock the magic within ourselves.

Whether you're a devoted reader of your daily horoscope or someone who barely comprehends their sun sign, this book is meant to be a guide on how to understand the influence that the planets have on your life and use them for your own highest good—from knowing your sun, moon, and rising signs, to learning what spells and rituals fit your sign. You will learn what the best spells are to cast during a full moon, and you will finally understand what a retrograde is anyway (and why it's so scary). While this book will not teach you everything there is to know about astrology, I hope that it gives you a better understanding on how to find magic within the stars, and how that magic influences your own.

So let the journey begin.

1

GETTING STARTED

While you may be familiar with your sun sign—the one you'd answer when someone asks what your sign is—you may be surprised to learn that you have several signs that make up who you are as a person. This is known as a natal or birth chart, and it holds key information on what makes you the witch you are today.

YOUR BIRTH CHART AND YOU

A birth chart is a snapshot of where the planets were the moment you came into this world. While learning your sun sign can help you understand one part of your personality, learning your whole birth chart can help you figure out the different sides of yourself: past, present, and future. This is especially true if you've never felt truly connected with your sun sign. Having your natal chart on hand will help you throughout this book, from learning about zodiac signs to understanding the astrological houses that influence your life. Fortunately, your birth chart isn't that hard to make.

Creating Your Birth Chart

Thanks to modern technology and the current popularity of astrology, creating your birth chart is simple. There are many free websites and apps that can generate your birth chart for you in a matter of seconds (see page 168). All you need is:

* The exact date you were born
* The exact time you were born
* The location where your birth took place

Accuracy is key here, especially with your birth time. Even being thirty minutes off could completely change your birth chart. So make sure you get the date, time, and location directly from your birth certificate.

What If You Don't Know Your Birth Time?

If you do not have access to your birth certificate or your birth certificate does not have the time on it, you still can create a birth chart; it just may not be as accurate—especially for your rising sign and astrological houses. You can try asking your parents your birth time for clues: if they remember it being early at night, before lunch, or even if it was a.m. or p.m. If you have no way of knowing, simply put down 12 p.m. in the generator, but remember that it may not be accurate.

Your Big Three

While every placement in your natal chart serves a certain purpose, there are three major placements you should pay attention to when first doing your chart: your sun, moon, and rising signs. This is known as your "big three" as they have the most influence on your life, representing core parts of your personality, your inner emotions, and how people see you as you go through life.

Sun Sign: Your Core Self

You probably already know this sign as it is the most recognizable sign in your chart. Since the sun moves through a particular sign every thirty days, the sun sign is calculated by the day you were born. Your sun sign represents who you are at your core, the type of person you are growing up to be. It shows how you express yourself, your life's purpose, and your basic personality traits. The sun shines its light on who you are destined to be.

Moon Sign: Your Emotional Self

Your moon sign represents your emotional self, how you *feel* about things, and the way you process emotions. It is your intuition, your instincts, and it can reveal where you find comfort and security. Representing our ever-changing moods, the moon moves through a zodiac sign every two and a half days. As the moon plays a big part in Wicca, you might say the moon sign is where your inner witch lives. At its core, your moon sign represents how you can best take care of yourself, and how you can tap into your inner powers.

Rising Sign: Others' Perceptions of You

Also known as the ascendant, the rising sign is one of the most important placements in the birth chart. It's the hardest to calculate because it comes from the astrological sign that was ascending the eastern horizon the exact moment you were born. So, if you don't have your birth time, you can't calculate your rising sign. Your ascendant represents how other people see you, how you come across to the world. It's also what motivates your actions and what drives you to do what you do.

Because the moon and rising signs move more quickly through a sign than the other planets, they can be very different from your sun sign or the other placements in your chart. This can explain why you act and feel so differently from your sun sign. It's good to keep these placements in mind as you work through this book.

Cleansing Your Space and Charging Your Tools

Throughout this book, there are plenty of spells, rituals, and tools that will help you with your cosmic practices. However, before you start casting, make sure that your space is cleansed, and your tools are charged, to ensure that your spells have the best chance of coming to fruition. You wouldn't make an important phone call with one percent of battery life, or invite new people over to a dirty house, right? So why would you do the same thing with magic?

Before we get started, let's go over basic cleansing and charging rituals.

Cleansing

Cleansing is the act of banishing negative energy from your space, your tools (crystals, herbs, candles, bowls, etc.), and even from yourself before casting. In order for spells to work their best, they need to work on a clean slate. That way, no negative influences can obstruct the success of your spell. It's important to cleanse your space before and after you cast a spell, especially if you are doing an intense ritual. Cleansing methods include:

* Taking a shower right before you cast.
* Taking a broom and "sweeping away" all the negative energy.
* Placing a bowl of salt next to where you're casting to dispel the negative energy.
* Spritzing a bottle of rose water in your space for protection and unconditional love.

Charging

Charging is the act of putting intentional energy into your tools, spells, and rituals to give them more power. Think of it as charging their vibrational energy like you would charge your phone. It's ideal to charge your tools right before casting your spells or to incorporate charging action while casting to give your spell an extra boost. Charging methods include:

* Putting your tools by the window under a full moon.
* Visualizing yourself putting energy into the tools that you are using.
* Dancing, singing, or just moving your body around to create positive energy.

Casting a Protective Circle

Before casting a spell or performing a ritual, you must first cast a circle of protection around yourself. Spell casting is a sacred act between yourself and the magic around you, and you must protect it—especially from outside and unwanted influences and spirits. By keeping your boundaries, you give your spell the best chance of manifesting—and keep yourself safe as well. There are a variety of ways to cast a circle, including:

✴ Close your eyes and visualize a circle of glowing, bright light surrounding you and your space. Visualize it until you can feel the vibrations within. Open your eyes and begin casting. When you are finished, close your eyes again and visualize the light slowly fading away until it disappears.

✴ Take some coarse table salt and pour it in a circle around the area you are working in. (Just remember to vacuum it all up once you're done!)

✴ Light four different candles (preferably one white, one red, one blue, and one green) and place them in the four directions of the room you are working in: white candle in the east, red candle in the south, blue candle in the west, and green candle in the north.

As you cast your circle, remember to invoke each of the four elements into your space.

> First turn to face the east and say:
>   "By the Air, I call upon you; grant me the power to communicate with the divine around me."
>   Then, face south and say:
>   "By the Fire, I call upon you; grant me the energy to create what I desire."
>   Then, face west and say:
>   "By the Water, I call upon you; grant me the emotional connection to sustain me."
>   Finally, face north and say:
>   "By the Earth, I call upon you; grant me the stability to stay grounded in this moment.

With the four elements at your disposal, you can start casting.

⭐ Safety Warning ⭐

This book makes use of candles, herbs, and essential oils in your casting practices. Please be careful when using candles and use best safety practices around fire. Do not consume any herbs or teas if you have allergies or do not know how those herbs might affect you. Stay safe, witches!

2

ZODIAC MAGIC

Hey witch, what's your sign? Even if you have the briefest understanding of what astrology is, you probably know your sun sign. However, just knowing that you're "a Pisces" or "a Virgo" doesn't give you the full story—both of who you are and astrology in general.

There are twelve astrology signs that make the wheel of the zodiac. In western astrology, the zodiac wheel makes up a calendar, where the sun moves throughout a sign every 30 days, representing the changes of the seasons, similar to the Wheel of the Year in Wicca. Much like the Wheel of the Year, the astrological calendar begins with the spring equinox. By learning more about astrology, you can begin to understand the world around you: how astrological changes can affect your magic, what type of spells to do at certain times, and the benefits and challenges each sign represents.

Learning more about your own sun, moon, and rising signs will also help you understand your own personal magic. The pages that follow give an overview of each zodiac sign and how you can harness them for your own magical practice: which crystals will help benefit your magic, which herbs can bring you comfort, and what magic you will be more drawn to.

Aries

COURAGEOUS ✳ PASSIONATE ✳ INDEPENDENT

SEASON: March 21–April 19
GLYPH: ♈
SYMBOL: The Ram
ELEMENT: Fire
MODALITY: Cardinal
PLANET: Mars
HOUSE: 1st House
BODY PARTS: Head and face
COLORS: Red, blood orange, yellow
WHEEL OF THE YEAR: Ostara (Vernal/Spring Equinox)

Bold, brash, and completely unafraid, Aries rams its way through life, starting both the Wheel of the Year and the Astrological New Year with a fiery passion and an independent attitude. As a cardinal sign, Aries is always trying to start something: from a fire to a fight. Ruled by Mars, Aries is ready for battle, even if the opponent is themselves. However, do not let this hot-headed, sometimes-reckless persona fool you; once you get through all that fire, there's a sensitive, almost childlike quality to the ram that makes them so easy to love. They feel everything so intensely that even a small joy makes them enthusiastic. It's why they get so enraged by any minor inconvenience. However, it's that intensity that makes Aries so magical.

Aries season begins on Ostara, the Wiccan holiday to celebrate the vernal or spring equinox. Ostara is named after the Germanic goddess of spring, celebrating harmony, fertility, and rebirth.

The spring equinox is the first of two times of the year when the number of daylight hours match the number of nighttime hours. After this moment, the days get a little warmer. Aries brings the heat to forge new creations.

Aries in the Natal Chart

If you have Aries somewhere in your big three, it can affect your magic and spiritual practice in unique ways—from finding your magic blooming more during the early spring, to having strong feelings about fire (either fascination or fear). Here's how Aries's magic shows up in your natal chart.

Aries Sun

An Aries sun's life purpose is to prove themselves through courageous acts. Most people think Aries are daredevils, recklessly ramming their way into dangerous situations without a safety net. While that may be true for some Aries, other Aries suns are looking for their own personal glories—whether they're breaking out of toxic generational cycles, being the first of their family to go to college, or being successful in their career. They are driven towards better horizons, often taking the lead for others to follow.

While their combative persona, blunt nature, and hot temper may burn more than a few bridges, Aries suns shine brightly when they are using their natural gifts to change the world: enthusiasm, confidence, optimism, and honesty. If you're an Aries sun, the lesson you will learn throughout your spiritual practice is that not every interaction is a duel that needs to be won. Peace can be the victory (so stop making hexes your "go-to" spell).

Aries Moon

There's a fire blazing in the heart of every Aries moon. The heat of their inner flame warms them when the world seems cold and motivates them forward when all seems lost. Blessed with an abundance of passion, enthusiasm, and courage, Aries moons need to take on new and exciting challenges in order to feel alive. Their comfort zone is right on the edge of danger, taking action, as they perform best when the stakes are high. It's the thrill of the chase that keeps them going. They feel safe when they have absolute freedom, a life free of restrictions and interference from authority figures. They need to burn freely, or they will torch the world or, worse, become extinguished.

At their best, an Aries moon witch is independent in their craft, optimistic in what they can achieve, and has an inner flame that burns brightly. At their worst, their magic is impulsive, they have a hard time waiting for their spells to manifest, and they burn their inner candle at both ends.

ARIES RISING

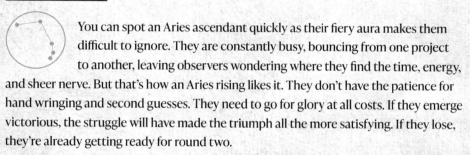 You can spot an Aries ascendant quickly as their fiery aura makes them difficult to ignore. They are constantly busy, bouncing from one project to another, leaving observers wondering where they find the time, energy, and sheer nerve. But that's how an Aries rising likes it. They don't have the patience for hand wringing and second guesses. They need to go for glory at all costs. If they emerge victorious, the struggle will have made the triumph all the more satisfying. If they lose, they're already getting ready for round two.

An Aries ascendant is a match; they can either be a guiding light in a dark world, or blow things up in a destructive blaze, depending on what strikes them at that moment. At first glance, An Aries seems to be looking for a fight with their independent, straightforward nature and a growing enemies list. However, once you get to know them, they are enthusiastic, courageous, and warm. An Aries ascendant witch may be drawn to fire magic, bold spell casting (especially creating their own spells on the spot), and may be solo witches if they cannot lead their own coven.

Aries and Magic

Aries placements can manifest their magic in unique ways, from starting important spells in the spring, to using their fiery passion to give their spells and rituals an extra boost. If you're looking to add a little of yourself or your energy into your craft, use these crystals, herbs, and areas of magic to give yourself a boost.

Crystals for Aries

 **BLOODSTONE:** The birthstone of Aries, bloodstone gives a major physical strength and helps calm your fears. Warriors would wear bloodstone on their arms to heal wounds and to keep them feeling courageous and strong. Keep a bloodstone crystal close to you when you're feeling ill to maintain your energy and heal you.

 **CARNELIAN:** As the stone of courage, carnelian gives off bold energy that both empowers the wearer and brings them plenty of joy and enthusiasm in whatever task they're doing. Carnelian brings inspiration and protection, which is perfect for leadership. Wear a carnelian necklace when you are about to take the lead or need a little extra courage in public.

 **RED JASPER:** As the stone of endurance, red jasper can help you as you go along your journey through life, giving you the strength to do good even when the chips are down. Wearing red jasper can bring the wearer an extra boost of energy, passion, and joy. Or, put a piece of this excellent motivator under your pillow at night. When you wake up, you'll feel more energized and ready to start the day.

Herbs for Aries

CAYENNE: Just like Aries, cayenne is hot, spicy, and sometimes difficult to handle. Cayenne peppers can be made into a fine powder that's used on food. While cayenne can add a much-needed kick to any dish, Aries placements will love its magical abilities: bringing protection, strength, motivation, and courage. Add some cayenne to your meal to remove any obstacles that are preventing you from what you want to achieve.

GINGER: This warm, stimulating herb has been used for centuries for its taste, healing benefits, and magical properties. While Aries placements usually reach for the caffeine, they should try drinking some ginger tea for an energy boost. Ginger also brings confidence, emotional balance, clarity, and some healing (perfect for those accident-prone Aries).

YARROW: A hardy perennial, you can find yarrow almost anywhere the sunshine is; the same could be said of Aries as well. In the Victorian language of flowers, yarrow represented both war and healing, and it was rumored to be used to heal warriors on the battlefield. Put some yarrow in a sachet to attract courage, psychic abilities, and love.

Best Type of Spells and Magic for Aries

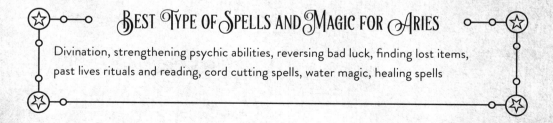

Divination, strengthening psychic abilities, reversing bad luck, finding lost items, past lives rituals and reading, cord cutting spells, water magic, healing spells

Anger is something that Aries placements know all too well—for their betterment and to their detriment. There are plenty of spells that talk about how to get rid of anger, but as any Aries placement knows, anger isn't always a bad thing. It can actually be the energy and drive needed to achieve great things. This spell will help transform your rage into the fire that drives you, not the fire that consumes you.

MATERIALS

- Red candlestick
- Candlestick holder
- Lighter
- Few pieces of paper
- Red ink pen
- Fireproof container
- Envelope

Optional:

- Candle snuffer

1 Place the candle in the candle holder and light it.

2 As you watch the flame of your candle, think about what is making you so angry. What or who is driving your rage?

3 On a piece of paper, write about what is making you so angry. Whether you're making an enemies list, venting about a situation you're in, or even scribbling and drawing angrily, let it all out!

4 When you're done, fold the paper in half. Put it towards the fire and burn a corner while saying, "Ashes to ashes, dust to dust, I feed the flame of my inner fire with justly rage. Soon my enemies will feel the burn."

5 Put the paper in the fireproof contain and watch it burn. While keeping a careful eye on the fire, take a second piece of paper and write out everything you want to achieve using this anger. Maybe you are facing an obstacle, or maybe someone told you that you couldn't achieve something. Write about your victory as if it has already happened.

6 When the paper has fully burned, put the snuffer in your hand, if using. Stand in front of the candle, and say, "Thank you for the fuel to light my ambitions. I will now light my own way. So mote it be," and put the candle out.

7 Put the second piece of paper in the envelope. When your candle has cooled, take it out of the holder and hold it over your envelope sideways. In your other hand, hold the lighter.

8 Use the lighter to light the end of the candle, heating it up so that the wax of the candle drips onto the envelope where you would typically seal it. As the wax drips, say "With my anger, I seal my faith. I will be victorious in my efforts to transform my life for the best. So mote it be."

9 Put the candle in a firesafe place to cool. Place the sealed envelope on your altar or carry it with you to help you on your way to victory.

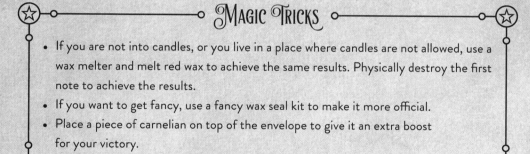

Magic Tricks

- If you are not into candles, or you live in a place where candles are not allowed, use a wax melter and melt red wax to achieve the same results. Physically destroy the first note to achieve the results.
- If you want to get fancy, use a fancy wax seal kit to make it more official.
- Place a piece of carnelian on top of the envelope to give it an extra boost for your victory.

TAURUS

RELIABLE ✷ TENACIOUS ✷ DEVOTED

SEASON: April 20–May 20
GLYPH: ♉
SYMBOL: The Bull
ELEMENT: Earth
MODALITY: Fixed
PLANET: Venus
HOUSE: 2nd House
BODY PARTS: Neck, shoulders, throat
COLORS: Green, pink, white
WHEEL OF THE YEAR: Beltane

The first earth sign on the astrological wheel, Taurus is the true embodiment of the element, a sign planted firmly in the ground, rooted in the physical realm. They are strong, sturdy, and have a stillness that allows them to appreciate the beauty of nature. Like the bull, they long to roam the pastures, taking in all the pleasures life has to offer.

Stubbornness is a defining trait of Taurus, and it is a double-edged sword. Like a glorious mountain, Taurus cannot be moved or pushed. They stand by their beliefs and the people they love with unwavering conviction. However, this stubbornness can also close them off to new opportunities and keep them stuck in vicious cycles. Taurus is a fixed sign; its season is in the middle of spring. However, Taurus must learn that seasons change, and so do we.

On the wheel of the year, the Sabbat holiday Beltane is held on May 1, in the middle of Taurus season. Beltane is the celebration of the God and Goddess coming together in physical union. During this time, the veil between the physical and the spiritual realm is at its thinnest, making it easy for fairies and elves to move back and forth. Taurus is the embodiment of all Beltane has to offer: sensual pleasure, romantic unions, and enjoying life.

Taurus in the Natal Chart

If you have Taurus in your big three, you may have a slow and steady approach to your craft. You may perform rituals that take a while to manifest but yield major results. You may also be drawn to herbalism, meditation, or just like making your altar beautiful. Here's how your Taurus energy manifests itself in different placements.

Taurus Sun

 A Taurus sun's life purpose is to enjoy the pleasures that life has to offer, from indulging in good food and wearing soft clothing, to feeling the sunlight on their skin. A Taurus sun knows that they only have one rare and precious life, and they are going to enjoy it. As an earth sign, they are willing to work hard in this life, but they work to live, not live to work.

Blessed with an abundance of patience, resourcefulness, and tenacity, the Taurus sun's magic may be slow-moving, but it is strong. You cannot push, force, or hurry a Taurus sun; they move at their own pace towards their destiny. They can manifest anything they desire as they have the diligence and endurance to plant the seeds and watch them grow. However, Taurus has a bossy side to them as well; they are inflexible and stubborn, with a possessive nature.

If you are a Taurus sun, your lesson for your spiritual practice is to become a little more flexible with your magic and step outside your comfort zone so you can become your most powerful self.

Taurus Moon

 A Taurus moon can endure any difficulty, but they must have stable and reliable comforts to feel emotionally secure. This isn't all eating chocolate cake for dinner or indulging in impulse retail therapy. It's the comfort of having a loving partner to build a life with. It's the security of having their own home. It's having the time and resources to watch a sunset or take a walk on the beach. Taurus moons need to take in the pleasures of life to sustain themselves. These are not people who operate on impulse. Instead, they soak in everything, thinking carefully before deciding. Because of this, people can depend on the Taurus moon. If a Taurus moon had it their way, they would have everyone they love under one roof. However, because of the Taurus moon's love of comfort, they can also be stuck in unhappy situations because they are too stubborn to change. Being flexible will always be a challenge.

At their best, the Taurus moon witch invests in their magic, tending to it regularly with patience, affection, and a steady flow of effort. They are someone other witches can trust. At their worst, they are possessive of magic, their coven, and tools, can be rigid in their rules and obstinate about their practice (even if it can be improved).

TAURUS RISING

 You can spot a Taurus ascendant by the way they dress. They have a classic, timeless aesthetic that they have cultivated throughout the years, often adorned with a statement necklace. Ruled by Venus, a Taurus rising knows a thing or two about beauty. They also have stellar social skills as people naturally flock to them because of their grounding, easygoing nature. While not party animals, a Taurus rising knows how to have a good time, from singing loudly at coven meetings to having a five-course meal with friends. However, their need for control and trying to force life to bend to their will can make them unhappy and kill the vibes. Above all else, a Taurus rising just wants to be building something that will last.

The Taurus ascendant first appears to be patient, artistic, and a little materialistic. However, once you get into their inner circle, you'll see that they are also steadfast, charming, and incredibly strong-willed. A Taurus rising witch approaches in a gentle way, often practicing daily rituals that help them manifest their dreams. They find happiness in covens where they can use their natural gifts to help others but will leave if they feel they are being pushed too hard.

TAURUS AND MAGIC

Taurus placements use their magic where they feel they will get the most benefit. They will plant gardens to grow herbs for money spells, they will make their altars beautiful so they will worship it daily, and they work slowly to perfect their craft. They are in magic for the long haul. If you're looking to add a little of yourself or your energy to your craft, use these crystals, herbs, and areas of magic to give yourself a boost.

CRYSTALS FOR TAURUS

EMERALD: The birthstone of Taurus, emerald is the stone of truth and love, perfect for this Venus-ruled sign. Emerald is also the stone of intuition. Wearing emerald can calm Taurus's fears about the future, if they had a glimpse of what's to come. Emerald brings success, good fortune, and financial gain. Wear an emerald ring while working with money or while working to bring more money to you.

MALACHITE: Being famous for their stubborn streak, fixed Taurus can be pretty resistant to change, often stuck in their own ways. Malachite can help Taurus break out of their comfort zone, calming their subconscious mind, and encouraging them to take risks—especially in business. Place a piece of malachite—with its abundance of healing, protection, and willpower—in your office if you are planning on making a major career change.

ROSE QUARTZ: The stone of unconditional love, rose quartz helps us develop stable relationships, something that Taurus placements crave. Rose quartz can help create a peaceful environment where everyone gets along but also creates peace and love within yourself. Put a rose quartz on your neck when you're having your next self-care day.

Herbs for Taurus

CARDAMON: A member of the ginger family, cardamon is a citrus-tasting spice that is often used in food and beverages. As the foodie of the zodiac, Taurus will already love making dishes using the spice but will also enjoy the magical benefits as well, including clarity, courage, direction, and lust. Make a dish featuring cardamon for a hot date if you want to get lucky.

ROSE: Ruled by Venus, Taurus is drawn to traditional romantic symbols, including roses. Roses are very important in witchcraft and can be used in multiple ways: rose oil, rosewater, rose tea, growing roses, etc. Taurus placements may find use in rose for calming down as well as for increasing their beauty, divination ability, and healing powers. Sip some rose tea before a big date to calm your nerves and bring out your inner beauty.

SAGE: From a typical kitchen herb to cleaning out bad vibes, Taurus placements should always keep common sage around for all of their magical needs. Different from white sage, common sage is often preferred in traditional Wiccan practices. Taurus placements can use sage for protection, wisdom, cleansing, longevity, and good luck. Write your wish on a sage leaf and sleep with it under your pillow for three days. On the third day, bury it in the garden for your wish to be granted.

Best Type of Spells and Magic for Taurus

Abundance spells, kitchen witchery, green witchery, singing bowl, spells for business success, love spells, musical rituals, healing magic, money manifesting, gardening

Taurus has an uncanny ability to manifest and attract what they desire in life because they have the patience and endurance to wait for the things they want to manifest. If you want to attract what you desire into your life, use music! Sound carries energy, and Taurus rules the throat and vocal cords that can be used for magic. So let's make some music. For this spell, you will need a singing or sound bowl, a bowl-shaped bell that produces sound when hit and circled with a small mallet. If you do not have a singing bowl, simply use music.

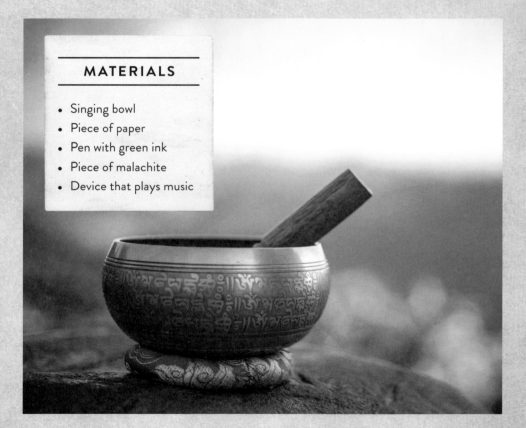

MATERIALS

- Singing bowl
- Piece of paper
- Pen with green ink
- Piece of malachite
- Device that plays music

1 Sit in a quiet place, preferably out in nature, but your bedroom will also work. Hit the side of the singing bowl with the mallet once, then use the mallet to circle the bowl three times, counterclockwise. This will cleanse the space and get rid of any negative energy. If you do not have a singing bowl, cleanse how you usually do.

2 On a piece of paper, write down what you wish to attract. Write as though you already have it, such as, "I'm grateful for my new home," "I love my partner; they are so sweet, calm, and steady." When you are finished, put the paper into the bowl and place the piece of malachite on top of the paper.

3 Choose a song that aligns with your intentions. It could be anything: from monks chanting to Stevie Nicks—whatever fits. Hit the singing bowl and use the mallet to circle it three times clockwise. Play the song.

4 Sing! Put your whole heart into it! It doesn't matter if you're a good singer or tone-deaf; sing it out! The magic comes from the passion you put into it, so sing, visualizing the magic moving from your body to the world.

5 In the middle of the song, hit the singing bowl again, circling it three times clockwise with the mallet. Keep singing.

6 As the song ends, hit the singing bowl once more, repeating what you have done before. Thank the elements and turn off the music.

7 Place the paper and malachite on your altar and continue on your day.

Magic Tricks

- Increase the vibrations by adding dance to your ritual.
- Bury your paper in your garden to speed up your intentions and have them come to be more quickly.
- Use the singing bowl whenever you need to cleanse crystals, herbs, or your space, as the sound can cleanse and heal the energy around them.

Gemini

SEASON: May 21–June 20
GLYPH: ♊
SYMBOL: The Twins
ELEMENT: Air
MODALITY: Mutable
PLANET: Mercury
HOUSE: 3rd House
BODY PARTS: Shoulders, lungs, arms, hands, fingers
COLORS: Light yellow, mint green, light blue
WHEEL OF THE YEAR: The transition from spring into summer

With the gift of gab and a fast-paced mind, Gemini wants to know everyone and everything. Their reputation may precede them for being inconsistent, flighty, and nosy, but it's Gemini who always gets the last word–and it's a zinger. However, while Gemini's clever quips can make them the star of any party, they are here to learn all the secrets. Because they are ruled by Mercury, the planet of communication, Geminis need to share everything they've learned, making them an asset in a coven–but a liability if they have dirt on you.

Symbolized by the twins, Geminis are often accused of talking out of both sides of their mouths. When Geminis change their mind, it's not because they are disloyal or lack convictions, but rather because they are so perceptive that they can see all sides of an issue. Their minds are so sharp and rational that they can easily see someone's point of view. Even if they don't agree, it keeps things interesting, and Gemini cannot stand to be bored.

Gemini season occurs during the transition from spring into summer. The seeds that we planted in the spring are starting to bloom, just like the seeds of information planted into Gemini become clever thoughts and ideas for the rest of us to harvest.

Gemini in The Natal Chart

If you have Gemini in your big three, you've probably spent a lot of time researching different parts of Wicca, divination, and astrology (it might be why you started reading this book!). You may bounce around from one type of practice to another, casting many spells at once. However, your way with words makes you gifted at spell crafting. Here's how your Gemini energy manifests itself in different placements.

Gemini Sun

A witch of all trades but a master of none, a Gemini sun has a variety of interests as they strive to learn a little bit about everything. Highly inquisitive and intelligent, Gemini sun can be the sharpest mind in the room; they can also be the local gossip if they don't get enough intellectual stimulation. Whatever the case may be, Gemini sun is eager to learn as well as share their knowledge with everyone.

Symbolized by the twins, Gemini suns are blessed with a dual nature, being able to use logic and intuition in their daily life. They can easily shift through what is fact and what is fiction. They are also gifted with conversational skills, creativity, and an adaptability that helps them fit in with any social circle. However, all that energy Gemini has is a nervous energy, coming off as scattered, flighty, and impressionable.

If you're a Gemini sun, your lesson throughout your spiritual practice is to think about the words you say before you speak them into being. You may not like what you've manifested in haste.

Gemini Moon

A mental sign in the emotional planet is quite the pairing as a Gemini moon needs to analyze their emotions rather than feel them. They soothe themselves by "talking it out," whether to a professional, a best friend, or even a stranger on the bus. Seekers of knowledge, their comfort zone is communicating with others, asking questions, and exchanging facts either vocally or through writing. They need to be around other people and share ideas to feel happy. Variety is the spice of life as a

Gemini moon thrives on constant change: new jobs, new locations, new friends. However, a Gemini needs to balance stimulation with stability to calm their sensitive nerves.

A Gemini moon witch's greatest strength is their mental quickness in spell crafting, their high energy, and natural charm that easily forms covens. Their magical weak spot is that they can be disorganized and inconsistent when it comes to their practice, making an uneasy flow of magic.

GEMINI RISING

 You'll probably hear a Gemini ascendant before you can see them. Excitable voice, rapid hand movements, and a mouth that's moving a mile-a-minute. Gemini always has something to say about any subject, whether they are sharing a little-known fact or asking a question. A Gemini rising is in constant motion, which can sometimes make them difficult to follow. They need constant mental stimulation and bounce from subject to subject, and social group to social group, giving them a restless appearance. However, a Gemini rising is just happiest when they are engaging in conversation with others. They need change and variety to keep things interesting. Gemini simply wants to tell their story to the world.

A Gemini rising first appears to be busy and witty, with excitability that can shift from nervous energy to coolness. However, if you can hold their attention long enough, you'll find that they are mentally quick, charming, and inquisitive. A Gemini ascendant witch will be drawn to all types of magic and covens with the goal of learning everything that Wicca has to offer. You will often find them at coven meetings with juicy gossip and a spell that will help you get a promotion.

Gemini and Magic

Gemini placements are usually witches who are jacks of all trades but masters of none. They have dabbled in almost every form of witchcraft but usually lose interest when they have to get invested. However, this is a blessing as your energetic nature can help you learn new magic methods quickly and with great enthusiasm. If you're looking to add a little of yourself to your craft, use these crystals, herbs, and areas of magic to give yourself a boost.

Crystals for Gemini

CITRINE: As the stone of success, citrine is perfect for those curious Gemini placements as it increases confidence, helps them focus, and broadens their minds so to increase their horizons. A lucky stone, citrine never needs to be cleansed because it naturally removes negative energy and can easily quell racing thoughts and anxiety. Put a piece of citrine on your desk while you work to bring extra success and knowledge.

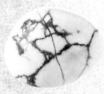

HOWLITE: Gemini is a high-energy sign, always bouncing from one subject to the next with passion and intensity. Howlite brings balance to this energy by giving Gemini some much-needed calming energy. Known as "the study stone," howlite can boost memory, increase reasoning skills, and help you stay objective on the pursuit of knowledge. Put a piece of howlite in your hand before a big meeting or class to help you really absorb the information.

TIGER'S EYE: Ruled by the Twins, Gemini placements can often be at odds with themselves over conflicting opinions and ideas. Luckily, tiger's eye is known for bringing balance to two extreme opposites, creating harmony. Tiger's eye also promotes courage, change, determination, and perseverance, helping flighty Gemini stick to their goals. Keep a piece of tiger's eye in your hand while deciding; it could lead you to the correct choice.

Herbs for Gemini

DILL: Often found in the kitchen, dill may help Gemini finally relax after a long day. From the old Norse word *dylla*, meaning "lull," dill has a soothing effect that can lean into feelings of safety and comfort. Magically, Gemini placements can use dill to bring vitality, pleasure, good luck, protection, and plenty of abundance. Plant some dill in your kitchen or garden to ensure you always have what you need.

LAVENDER: The universal healing herb, lavender is just as flexible as Gemini, soothing any part of the body that needs it—including the mind and the spirit. Like Gemini, lavender has a dual nature as it can be stimulating with its pleasing floral scent as well as relaxing. For Gemini placements, lavender can help them gain clarity, reduce worry, and bring balance to their mind and body. Spritz some lavender spray in your space before working, communicating, creating, or casting to ground yourself and bring peaceful intentions into the room.

PEPPERMINT: With its notable minty taste, peppermint not only promotes good oral health but may also soothe the headaches that Geminis get from overthinking. Next to the strong healing properties, Geminis are drawn to peppermint for its cleansing ability, psychic properties, protection, and energy renewal. Drink some peppermint tea after a stressful day to have good dreams.

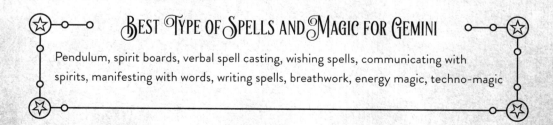

Best Type of Spells and Magic for Gemini

Pendulum, spirit boards, verbal spell casting, wishing spells, communicating with spirits, manifesting with words, writing spells, breathwork, energy magic, techno-magic

Geminis have a wide appetite for knowledge, but sometimes they
don't have enough focus to commit to studying and learning a subject.
Whether you're trying to remember important details for a test or need
to concentrate, this spell will help Gemini gain enough self-discipline
to focus on anything with success.

MATERIALS

- Two yellow candles
  with a long burn
  time (representing
  enlightenment)
- Two candle holders (if
  candles are not in jars)
- 1 citrine crystal
- 1 howlite crystal
- 1 tiger's eye crystal
- Lighter or matches
- Whatever you're
  reading/trying to
  focus on
- Candle snuffer

1 Set up where you usually study, free of any clutter and distraction, preferably at a desk or table where you can sit down. Cleanse the area.

2 Place the two candles on the table with the citrine, hoplite, and tiger's eye in the space between them.

3 Light the first candle and say, "With this flame, I light the spark of ideas. Let the flame invigorate my mind and allow my thoughts to be clear, steadfast, and creative."

4 Light the second candle and say, "With this flame, I light the flame of concentration. Let the flame guide my best intuition and give me focus, will, and discipline to reach my intellectual goals. So mote it be."

5 Work on whatever you are studying or project that you are doing (do not leave the candles unattended). When you are finished, take your snuffer and say, "Thank you for the gift that you have given me," while snuffing out each candle.

6 Repeat when needed.

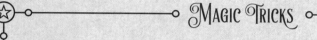

Magic Tricks

- For best results, perform this spell on a Wednesday (ruled by Mercury, the planet of intellect) or Saturday (ruled by Saturn, the planet of discipline).
- Light peppermint-scented candles to increase your focus.
- Brew some lavender tea to drink during this spell to boost clarity.

CANCER

NURTURING ✴ EMPATHIC ✴ SENTIMENTAL

SEASON: June 21–July 22
GLYPH: ♋
SYMBOL: The Crab
ELEMENT: Water
MODALITY: Cardinal
PLANET: The Moon
HOUSE: 4th House
BODY PARTS: Chest and stomach
COLORS: Blue, white, sea green
WHEEL OF THE YEAR: Litha (the Summer Solstice)

Get ready for the *feels*. Cancer brings us to the deep waters of emotion, from our most cherished childhood memories to our most haunted wounds. Cancer remembers it all. Cancer is not afraid to be vulnerable, but they do have a keen survival instinct. Much like the crab that symbolizes it, Cancer does not walk around with their heart on their sleeves. They have a hard outer layer of moodiness and defensiveness that everyone has to get through. But past that hard shell is the soft tenderness that is Cancer, the natural caregiver, the protective friend, and the imaginative lover. Cancer must protect their most treasured gift: an empathic heart.

Cancer season begins on Litha, the Wicca holiday celebrating the summer solstice and the victory of the Holly King against the Oak King. This is a time of abundance, growth, and magic.

It might seem strange to have Cancer, a sign ruled by the moon, start its season on the longest day of the year. However, the sun sets a little earlier each day after that, as Cancer slowly gets closer to its precious moon. This perfectly represents Cancer's dedication, love, and private devotion.

Cancer in the Natal Chart

If you have Cancer in your big three you may have noticed that your magic usually comes from emotions. If you're in a good mood, you can cast the most potent spell. However, if you're in a negative mood, you can make the most damaging hex. Here's how your Cancer energy manifests itself in different placements.

Cancer Sun

 A Cancers sun's life purpose is to form emotional bonds with others. These are people with strong roots. They want a home, they want a family (whether by blood or by bond), and they want to feel that love around them always. Cancer suns are sensitive souls, even if they don't want people to know their soft and tender spots, and they simply want to love and be loved in return.

The Goddess gifts Cancer suns with intuitive wisdom, kindness, protectiveness, and an empathic heart. They are the ones to go to when you need nonjudgmental advice, a shoulder to cry on, and the best chicken noodle soup you've ever had. Cancer loves to put on the caretaker role, but when they become drained by users and energy vampires, they can become moody, overly sensitive, and completely shut down in order to heal.

If you're a Cancer sun, the lesson for your spiritual practice is that your vulnerability is both a strength and a weakness. Setting boundaries can help protect yourself and your magic without locking people out.

Cancer Moon

 The natal moon in Cancer is the strongest placement that the crab can be in, but also the most vulnerable. A Cancer moon feels the ebbs and flows of emotional life, similar to the waning and waxing of the moon. Because of their sensitivity, they need a safe place to call their home, one where they are taken care of and have people to take care of. Loyal and protective, they will do anything for the people they love, even sacrificing themself in the process. Cancer moons can easily get lost in the sea of nostalgia; holding onto the past can either be a life raft or an anchor to them. It is their job to let their strong feelings motivate them without destroying them.

At their best, a Cancer moon witch uses their natural empathy to heal others and their strong intuition for divination purposes, and they are tirelessly devoted to their coven and craft. However, their weak spots are their moodiness (which can affect the potency of their spells), their use of magic for manipulation, and their hypersensitivity to the moods of others.

Cancer Rising

 Cancer ascendants have impeccable emotional memory when it comes to others. Natural empaths, they'll probably know more about you after the first meeting than you know about them. They know how you take your coffee, what colors you're drawn to, and your mother's name. They can feel the emotions of others easily and are often drawn to those who are struggling the most. A Cancer rising wants to be known for their ability to take care of others. However, the emotional labor a Cancer rising takes on can be taxing and they can easily take the slight word or tone of voice personally because of their heightened sensitivity. They need time to wade in their own emotions before they can take on the emotions of others.

When you first meet a Cancer rising, they can come across as moody, reserved, defensive, and very shy. However, once you spend more time with them, you'll discover they are kind, imaginative, loving, and giving. A Cancer ascendant witch may be drawn to divination, aura readings, and lunar magic. They treat their coven like they are family.

Cancer and Magic

If you have Cancer in your big three, your magic and your emotional states are forever intertwined, and knowing that can help you step into your personal power. You need to have your emotions work for you, not against you. The power of the moon can help. If you're looking to add a little of your energy into your craft, use these crystals, herbs, and areas of magic to give yourself a boost.

Crystals for Cancer

MOONSTONE: Often referred to as the birthstone of Cancer, moonstone is often associated with the lunar-ruled planet. In ancient times, moonstone was carried by people traveling at night to keep them safe from harm. Moonstone helps improve intuition, connecting to the subconscious, and aids in self-expression—perfect for Cancers who have a hard time speaking up for themselves about their own wants and needs. Keep a piece of moonstone on a key chain to keep you safe.

OPAL: Associated with water planets because of its high water content, opal is a healing crystal, helping transform negative energy into positive energy within one's self. For Cancers who like to hang onto the past—especially grudges—opal can help shine a light on the good memories. Keep a piece of opal near family photographs so you always remember the good.

SELENITE: Like moonstone, selenite is also associated with the moon, named after Selene, the Greek moon goddess. Selenite can cleanse the mind of negative thoughts and boost Cancer placements' intuition, the ability to forgive, and self-discovery. Selenite also can offer some needed protection. Hold a piece of selenite when meditating to calm the mind.

Herbs for Cancer

ALOE: Aloe and Cancer have a lot in common: they both have a sharper outside, but a healing, gooey inside. Aloe is an ancient healing plant that has been used for generations to heal burns, soothe stomachs, and banish bad luck. Aloe also brings beauty, love, and abundance and is very beneficial in moon magic. Keep an aloe plant in your kitchen to prevent any accidents.

CHAMOMILE: A key ingredient in our favorite sleepy-time teas, chamomile provides the comfort Cancer placements need after a long day of taking care of other people. Chamomile brings money, peace, love, tranquility, beauty, healing, and luck. Drink some chamomile tea before bed for restful, healing dreams.

LEMON BALM: Another tea-time favorite, lemon balm is often referred to as the "elixir of life" by herbalists for its healing qualities, energy renewal, and longevity. Cancer placements will enjoy lemon balm for bringing love, dreams, confidence, happiness, prosperity, sensuality, and dreamwork into their lives. Dry lemon balm leaves and add them to a sachet to carry with you, place on your altar, or place under your pillow to bring love into your life.

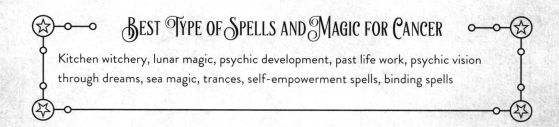

Best Type of Spells and Magic for Cancer

Kitchen witchery, lunar magic, psychic development, past life work, psychic vision through dreams, sea magic, trances, self-empowerment spells, binding spells

Cancer placements have huge hearts and incredibly empathic souls. However, it's because of these traits that they tend to attract toxic people and absorb their energy. If you've been tired, unwell, or moodier than usual, it may be time to cleanse yourself of the negative vibes you picked up from people by scrubbing it away.

MATERIALS

- Large bowl
- Spoon
- 2 cups Epsom salts (cleansing the energy)
- ¾ cup coconut oil (cleansing the spirit)
- 5 drops chamomile essential oil (comfort and inner healing)
- 5 drops lemon essential oil (energy, healing, and confidence)
- Airtight container

1 In the bowl, mix together the Epsom salts and coconut oil. Add the chamomile and lemon oils and continue to stir clockwise until well combined.

2 As you stir, say, "With this mixture, I call upon the spirits and the elements that protect me to heal my aura and cleanse my energy from the negativity I have absorbed. Whenever I use this scrub, I am washing away the bad and opening myself up for only good things. So mote it be."

3 If you don't plan on using the scrub right away, put it in an airtight container until you are ready to use.

4 When you are ready to use, get in your shower or bath, and put the scrub on your body, working it into your skin in a counterclockwise motion. As you wash, visualize in your mind all the negativity that is leaving you.

5 When you are fully clean, step out of the bath and get dressed. Be gentle with yourself for the rest of the day.

Magic Tricks

- For best results, preform this spell on a Monday (associated with the moon).
- For extra magic, do this at night during a waning moon. After using the scrub, walk outside and meditate under the glow of the moon to soak in some of its power.
- If you need some extra healing, add a cup of aloe vera gel to your mix.
- You can also use dried chamomile and dried lemon balm in your scrub if you prefer.

Leo

VIBRANT ✴ PLAYFUL ✴ LOYAL

SEASON: July 23–August 22
GLYPH: ♌
SYMBOL: The Lion
ELEMENT: Fire
MODALITY: Fixed
PLANET: The Sun
HOUSE: 5th House
BODY PARTS: Heart, spine, upper back
COLORS: Orange, gold, purple
WHEEL OF THE YEAR: Lammas/Lughnasadh

Look out, witches, the star has arrived! Leo is always looking for the spotlight, and why shouldn't they? They are ruled by the biggest, brightest star in the sky: the sun! However, don't let Leo's flair for dramatics and regal aura about them fool you. Leos have generous hearts, creative minds, and are completely faithful. Leos do not want a lot—just to be loved (by everyone in the world).

All the world's a stage, and no one knows that better than Leo. Every day is a chance to put on a performance: from giving it their all in a presentation to putting on a complete outfit to pick up milk. Leo wants to make the world a brighter, happier, and better place, but whatever good Leo does, they want credit in return, which gives them the reputation of being vain, overbearing, and selfish. However, Leo always has the best intentions at heart.

On the Wheel of the Year, the Wicca Sabbat, Lammas (also known as Lughnasadh), is celebrated on August 1, in the middle of Leo season. On Lammas, we celebrate abundance, creativity, and gratitude for a bountiful harvest season, all traits that are associated with the generous lion who treats each day like a celebration.

Leo in the Natal Chart

If you have Leo in your big three, your magic shines a little more brightly than the other placements. You believe that casting and rituals should be grand performances where you are the star attraction. You may be drawn to fire magic, large rituals, divination, and large coven meetings. You may really dive into the whole "witch" persona for fun and excitement. Here's how your Leo energy manifests itself in different placements.

Leo Sun

A Leo sun's life purpose is to burn brightly and share their natural joy, passion, and radiance with the world. Natural performers, Leo suns are always stealing the show and the hearts of everyone. By commanding the hearts and minds of others, a Leo sun can truly find their place in the world—and have a good time doing it.

Gifted with warmth, bravery, and a playful attitude, Leo sun believes they should treat each day like a celebration. While they love a good party, Leo sun isn't lazy. They work hard to make everyone happy, providing creative ideas, laughs, and even romance to keep things hot. However, they can easily turn to dramatics, domineering behavior, self-obsession, and bitterness—especially if they don't get the attention they crave. Leo is truly giving but needs a little love in return.

If you're a Leo sun, the lesson for your spiritual practice is to celebrate yourself and your magic fully. Don't wait for the applause of others. You are a powerful witch, and you know it.

Leo Moon

With the heart of a lion, Leo moons have strong emotions that motivate their actions through life. To change their mind, you need to change how they feel about a situation. Above all else, a Leo moon needs positive attention, acknowledgment, and, yes, even applause to feel safe and secure. Even Leo moons who have an uncomfortable time in the spotlight need to feel appreciated to find happiness. They need to express their creativity and to actively feel their most authentic self. Every day to a Leo moon is an exciting adventure, and if they cannot find excitement and joy, they are more than happy to create it. Action-oriented and natural leaders, Leo moons are here to put on a show—from showbiz personalities to public leaders. Their hearts and emotions belong to all.

At their best, Leo moon witches are deeply creative when it comes to their magic and rituals; they make even the driest Wicca ritual fun. They bring exuberant energy to each spell they cast. However, they can be pretty bossy and overbearing at coven meetings and can be tempted to use their magic for personal gain.

Leo Rising

 The first thing one may notice about a Leo ascendant is their amazing head of hair. Like the mane of the lion they symbolize, a Leo ascendant wears their hair like a crown, making people stand up and take notice. You'll generally find a Leo rising at the center of attention, as that's their favorite place to be. Even if they don't seek out the attention of others, people will flock to them as they radiate fun, warmth, and vibrant energy from their powerful presence. They are the happiest when they are the leader of any situation, taking the stage and taking charge. They want to be known for the joy they give to others and know they are leaving their mark on the world.

Leo ascendants first appear to be charming, influential, and confident but boastful. However, once you spend some time with them, you'll discover they are generous, idealistic, passionate, and big hearted. Leo ascendant witches are often the first ones you see volunteering to lead the coven in rituals, especially if it involves fire and flare.

Leo and Magic

If you have Leo in your big three, you probably take a more dramatic approach to your craft, complete with tools, tarot readings, and a robe to wear while casting. As a witch, you know that performance is part of the craft, and you love putting on a show. If you're looking to add more tailored props to your performance, use these crystals, herbs, and rituals.

Crystals for Leo

 **PYRITE:** Nicknamed "fool's gold," pyrite is associated with the element of fire, bringing passion and energy within. Leo placements can use pyrite when they need help removing creative barriers as it manifests prosperity and encourages authenticity and creativity. Keep a pyrite cluster on your desk to attract new opportunities and prosperity.

 **RUBY:** One of the birthstones associated with Leo, ruby is also the stone of nobility for the powerful vibrations that it gives off—similar to the vibes Leo placements tend to give off. Ruby is a powerful grounding crystal used to bring courage, strength, fortitude, and a lust for life. When life gets hard, put on a ruby ring and keep going.

 **SUNSTONE:** Named after Leo's ruling planet, it's said that sunstone gets its vibrant, joyful energies directly from the sun's rays. As the stone of leadership, sunstone helps Leo placements embrace their personal power, establish emotional connections with others, and take responsibility. Wear a sunstone crown when you're ready to take charge.

Herbs for Leo

CALENDULA: Also known as pot marigold, calendula brings opportunities to help the fixed Leo placements get out of their ruts and bring new opportunities for change and growth. Calendula brings warm, gentle energies that nurture us and bring us opportunities for wealth, love, and positive energy. Put some calendula petals in a bath to draw admiration from others and give you a sunny glow.

ST. JOHN'S WORT: Often gathered during Midsummer (during Leo season), St. John's wort brings happiness, love, protection, and strength and is often used in dream magic, protection spells, and to banish negative energy. Dry some St. John's Wort and hang it in the window to protect yourself from fire, lightning, ghosts, and misfortune.

SUNFLOWER: Associated with good luck, truth, and joy, the sunflower is the flower of loyalty, as it follows the sun from east to west every day. Plant some sunflowers in the front of your home to bring positive energy to your space.

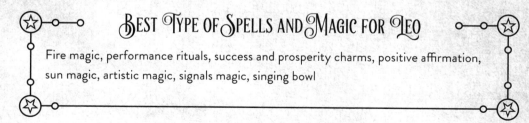

Best Type of Spells and Magic for Leo

Fire magic, performance rituals, success and prosperity charms, positive affirmation, sun magic, artistic magic, signals magic, singing bowl

For the bold and dramatic Leo placements, every spell and ritual should act like a performance. What is the point of being a witch if you aren't going to have fun with it? Here is a general way of spell casting that will feed Leo's need for movement and putting on a show—even if it's just for themselves.

MATERIALS

- Space to move around in
- Costume (a wild outfit that sparks your inner witch, or just something that makes you feel good)
- Firm intention in mind

Optional:

- Candles (preferably representing the earth, water, fire, and air)
- Audience
- Music
- Altar with pyrite, ruby, and sunstone

1 Set your "stage." This can be an actual stage (if you have that kind of permission), or it can be alone in your bedroom. If working with candles, they should be in a place where they will not get knocked over. If you're working with crystals or an altar, set them up now.

2 When your stage is set, put on your "costume." This can be any outfit that makes you feel good or part of your spell. You can bring out your inner witch with a total witchy outfit, you can dress in pink and red if you are trying to attract love, or you can even dress in your interview outfit if this is a job spell. Whatever feels good and right.

3 If you prefer an audience, bring them in now, either in real life or on video chat. Invite your coven to watch the show.

4 Stand in the center of the room, hands to your side and feet firmly on the ground. Close your eyes and imagine the outcome you want this spell to bring: a new job, a lover, money, fame, whatever. Picture it in your mind. If you have music, now is the time to turn it on.

5 Dance! Move your body to the rhythm of the spell you are creating in your mind. This doesn't have to be perfectly choreographed or even good dancing. Just move your body! If you are using sigil magic (a symbol created and drawn with magical intention), dance in the pattern of the sigil you are trying to cast. Call upon the elements if you wish. However, above all else, let yourself be free. Sing. Recite your favorite movie lines. Whatever feels good in this moment, do it.

6 When you are done, take a bow towards the four directions (east, south, west, north) to show your thanks, and then close the circle.

Virgo

HELPFUL ✷ PRACTICAL ✷ DILIGENT

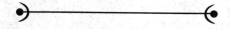

SEASON: August 23–September 22
GLYPH: ♍
SYMBOL: The Maiden
ELEMENT: Earth
MODALITY: Mutable
PLANET: Mercury
HOUSE: 6th House
BODY PARTS: The digestive tract
COLORS: Navy, brown, olive green
WHEEL OF THE YEAR: Transition from summer into fall

Symbolized by the maiden, Virgo is a priestess, appearing all-knowing as they guide their coven into their magical destinies. You can usually find them pouring over their grimoires, practicing and perfecting their sacred rituals, and studying by candlelight. Virgo does not seek the leadership position, but they are the first person we come to when we need advice, help, and a certain set of skills that only the Maiden Priestess can provide. Virgo thrives on being helpful; they work hard on gaining a variety of different skills and information to best be of help. They find purpose in the act of service.

Virgos can often come off as cold, distant, and critical, but that isn't a fair assessment. Virgo usually stays separate from the group, as their job is behind the scenes. They are constantly studying, analyzing, and calculating what everyone needs so they can best provide. That's how they show their love.

Virgo season occurs during the transition from summer into fall. Virgo watches the leaves change colors and gathers what is useful from the beautiful summer and saves it for the autumn ahead.

Virgo in The Natal Chart

If you have Virgo in your big three, you have a methodical approach when it comes to your craft. You may try doing a spell twice: once by the book and once with your own personal improvements to make the spell perfect. You may be drawn to more "practical" forms of magic such as herbalism, kitchen magic, tea spells, and daily rituals. Here's how your Virgo energy manifests itself in different placements.

Virgo Sun

 A Virgo sun's life purpose is to be working on something meaningful. Virgos are incredibly hard workers and can easily become workaholics. However, for a Virgo sun to be truly happy, they need to be working on something that has tangible value. Whether they're doctors healing the sick, researchers unlocking the mysteries of the universe, writers telling their stories, or witches working with their craft–they are all working towards a goal, and it is that work where they find meaning.

The Goddess has gifted Virgo suns with practicality, diligence, efficiency, and a quick wit that makes them quite charming–which can ease some of the hurt feelings when Virgo sun's judgement, hypercritical opinions, and fussiness come out. Virgo perfectionism is both a strength and a flaw. They want things to be the best they can be but will tear themselves and others into pieces pointing out flaws–real or imagined. It is their mission to try to balance their desire to get things done perfectly rather than just getting them done right.

If you're a Virgo sun, the lesson for your spiritual practice is to learn how to master your craft without it consuming you.

Virgo Moon

 A Virgo moon handles emotions the same way they handle every other aspect of life: methodically. They are probably one of the best people to come to in a crisis as they handle even the most difficult situations with rationality and practicality, and they are creative enough to come up with unique solutions. It is outside of crisis mode where Virgo feels uneasy, where every minor inconvenience is cause for distress.

For a Virgo moon, they don't need just a backup plan to feel comfortable; they need a backup plan to their backup plan. They are also seekers of knowledge, gaining information for them to use in their daily life. Virgo moon isn't afraid of hard work; they actually feel their best when they feel useful, though they may obsess over the smallest detail.

At their best, Virgo moon witches use their magic to help others; they are steadfast in their natural magical flow and are a natural at spell writing. At their worst, their nervous energy affects their magic, and they can be critical and judgmental with their coven members.

Virgo Rising

 You may not notice a Virgo rising at first glance, but they'll be sure to notice you. While not the center of attention at parties or social gatherings, they are outside the circle, watching and analyzing everyone. Even before you talk to them, they probably already know your name, your job, and what you like to drive, based on what they picked up by simply observing. You can usually find them deep in thought as they study the room or take charge behind the scenes, making sure everything gets done and gets done *right*. Virgo rising has a reputation of being a perfectionist, highly critical of all flaws. However, a Virgo rising just wants to be known for mastering their area of expertise, from being a skilled writer to making the best apple pie. If they are successful at what they put effort into, they shine like a star.

Virgo risings first appear to be shy, cold, and overly critical. But when they finally warm up to someone, you'll see how helpful, kind, and absolutely witty they can be. A Virgo ascendant witch may be drawn to magical practices that help ground their anxious mind and perform the usual functions of daily life.

Virgo and Magic

If you need a spell written quickly, call a Virgo placement, as they always have one ready. While Virgos can best use their energy in the written word, they can also use their practical nature to analyze books about Wicca and use the best practices in their craft. Use these crystals, herbs, and rituals to boost your own craft.

Crystals for Virgo

AMAZONITE: The stone of communication, amazonite is an earthy stone that was named after the Amazon River and helps bring soothing energies, something that would greatly benefit Virgo's anxious, obsessive energy. Amazonite can help Virgo placements embrace imperfection and cultivate a sense of self-love and compassion. Wear an amazonite necklace to soothe your anxiety when sharing your thoughts.

MOSS AGATE: When the serious Virgo needs to open up, they should get a piece of moss agate, a natural calming stone that can unlock their emotional side and help them get in touch with their feelings. It's also a great crystal for goal setting, self-improvement, and some much-needed encouragement. Place a piece of moss agate on your altar to help you achieve your goals.

PERIDOT: One of the birthstones associated with Virgo, the peridot is the ultimate energy cleanser, cleaning the body, mind, and spirit of negativity–something that the tidy Virgo can really appreciate. Peridot represents rebirth, growth, and healing as it opens the heart and mind. Wear a peridot bracelet for success.

Herbs for Virgo

CORNFLOWER: In one of the most beautiful shades of blue, cornflower is stunning to look at. It also has a variety of magical benefits that Virgo placements can use in their daily life, including the enhancement of psychic abilities, self-knowledge, abundance, love, and creativity. Boil the petals and use it as ink to write out your spells and manifestations, or use it for automatic psychic writing rituals (free writing for the purpose of divination).

LICORICE ROOT: Licorice root is one of the world's oldest herbal remedies, but it doesn't taste like the candy (which is actually flavored with anise). Licorice root is often used for various healing rituals that can soothe the health-conscious Virgo. The herb is also associated with lust, passion, love, binding, and control. Make some tea with licorice to drink while working on your goals to help you tap into your personal power.

SKULLCAP: Despite its spooky name, skullcap is an excellent comforting herb to put your mind at ease by promoting peace and calm. Skullcap is often used for binding spells and to help stay grounded in any situation. Put some skullcap in your pillow for some relaxation before bed.

Best Type of Spells and Magic for Virgo

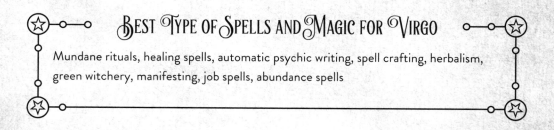

Mundane rituals, healing spells, automatic psychic writing, spell crafting, herbalism, green witchery, manifesting, job spells, abundance spells

Virgo placements need rituals and routines in order to be at peace in this life. However, unlike Leo, who needs flair when it comes to their performances, Virgo is more than happy to work in the mundane. Here is a simple tea ritual to do every morning that will clarify and calm a Virgo's day so they can get started on the right foot.

MATERIALS

- ½ cup black tea
- ¼ cup dried cornflower
- ⅛ cup dried skullcap
- ⅛ cup dried licorice root
- Medium airtight jar
- Teaspoon
- Teacup
- Tea infuser

1 Gather the tea, cornflower, skullcap, and licorice root in front of the jar.

2 Take the black tea in your hand and say, "With this black tea, I call upon the spirits to give me clarity, energy, and a steady place to ground myself each day." Pour it into the jar. Take the cornflower and say, "With this dried cornflower, I call upon the spirits to give me an abundance of creativity and physic vision." Pour it into the jar. Take the skullcap and say, "With this skullcap, I call upon the spirits to ground me and relax me through my day." Pour it into the jar. Finally, take the licorice root and say, "With this licorice root, I call upon the spirits to help me gain control over my life and help me find my own power." Pour it in.

3 With the spoon, mix the herbs while saying, "With the power of the elements, I drink this blend to give myself the strength, clarity, and nurturing that I deserve. With each sip, I am getting closer to my practice and my best self." Close the jar.

4 The next morning, get your favorite cup and put a tablespoon of the tea blend into your tea infuser. Prepare the tea, as usual, thinking about the day ahead.

5 When your tea is made, stir it three times, clockwise, saying, "With this brew, I will start my day clear, grounded, and wise," with each stir.

6 Drink the tea quietly as you get ready to start your day. Repeat every morning.

✦ Magic Tricks ✦

- If you want to practice divination each morning, skip the infuser, pour loose tea into your cup, and drink it that way. When you are finished, give yourself a tea reading.
- As you drink your tea, meditate and visualize the day ahead.
- If you are not a tea drinker, perform the same ritual with coffee.

LIBRA

ROMANTIC * CHARMING * FAIR

SEASON: September 23–October 22
GLYPH: ♎
SYMBOL: The Scales
ELEMENT: Air
MODALITY: Cardinal
PLANET: Venus
HOUSE: 7th House
BODY PARTS: Kidneys, lumbar region, skin
COLORS: Light pink, light blue, lavender
WHEEL OF THE YEAR: Mabon (the Fall Equinox)

Blessed by grace, charm, and a glamour that easily attracts others, Libras have a star power that is quite unmatched. They are gifted with social graces, with the perfect amount of charm to make them instantly likable—mainly because they are wise enough to keep their mouths shut (unless the situation calls for it).

However, do not mistake this Venus-ruled sign to be just a pretty face. They are driven by their need for fairness and harmony. They cannot stand to see an injustice done and will do everything in their power to put things right. This is why it takes so long for them to make a decision; they are so afraid of making the wrong or unfair choice that they will agonize over it. They need to study, think, and talk to all sides before coming to a reasonable decision.

Libra season begins on Mabon, the Wicca holiday to celebrate the autumn equinox. This equinox perfectly represents Libra's desire for balance, as daytime and nighttime are the same length. On Mabon, we celebrate the second harvest and reflect on what we have learned and grown. It is a time of having fun but also preparing for the winter ahead. Libra can enjoy the moment but also gather what they need for the future.

LIBRA IN THE NATAL CHART

If you have Libra in your big three, your craft has a more aesthetic approach. You want things to be beautiful, from your altar to what your spell looks like (they need to have an "Instagram worthy" quality). Here's how your Libra energy manifests itself in different placements.

LIBRA SUN

 A Libra sun's life purpose is to bring beauty and harmony to this world. These are our artists, our creators, but they are also our judges, lawyers, diplomats, and our matchmakers. Brewing up love potions and glamour spells, a Libra sun just wants to make everyone happy and feeling their best self.

A Libra sun shines best when they are willing to meet people halfway on a subject. They solve most of their problems quickly by just being willing to compromise. They are willing to listen to anyone's point of view and are happy to make a decision that works in everyone's best interests. Though Libra suns can be people-pleasing, vain, indecisive, and codependent, at their best they are thoughtful, peaceful, charming, and idealistic.

If you're a Libra sun, the lesson for you throughout your spiritual practice is to find ways to use your magic to shine in your own radiant light.

LIBRA MOON

 A Libra moon is more even-tempered than most signs in the moon. They have an emotional intelligence and cool logic that prevents them from flying off the handle in emotional fits of passion. However, what they cannot stand is conflict. They can intuitively sense when things are out of balance, which causes them great anxiety. They need to make peace, to create harmony, even at great cost. However, their personal charm and natural diplomacy makes it easy for them to get along with everyone. For a Libra moon to be happy, they need to be surrounded by beauty. Whether they are making art, buying furniture, or dressing in a stylish outfit, they are soothed when they are around things that look good and feel good.

At their best, Libra moon witches are adaptable in their craft, take an artistic approach to spells, and use their charms to win over coven members. At their worst, they can be dependent on other witches, have a hard time deciding on a spell, and can be a little frivolous.

Libra Rising

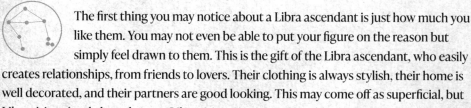

The first thing you may notice about a Libra ascendant is just how much you like them. You may not even be able to put your figure on the reason but simply feel drawn to them. This is the gift of the Libra ascendant, who easily creates relationships, from friends to lovers. Their clothing is always stylish, their home is well decorated, and their partners are good looking. This may come off as superficial, but Libra rising simply loves beauty. Libra risings are very agreeable, as peace and harmony are their main motivators. Their key phrase is, "Oh, I'm good with whatever you want to do." They will happily nod their head when someone is talking, even when they don't agree. If an argument occurs, they will do whatever it takes to stop it, from providing distractions to physically leaving the situation.

When you first meet a Libra rising, you may consider them to be attractive, charming, sociable, but a major people-pleaser and a little shallow. However, once you get to know them, you'll discover that they are fair-minded, artistic, and optimistic. A Libra ascendant witch will be drawn to glamour spells, spells that involve teamwork, and rituals that bring lots of love.

Libra and Magic

Libra placements can manifest their magic by working together with a trusted magical partner. They often use their magic to help keep their lives balanced and create harmony. If you're looking to add some of yourself to your craft, try these crystals, herbs, and rituals.

Crystals for Libra

AMETRINE: For the Libra placements who simply cannot make up their mind, ametrine is the best of both worlds, a blend of citrine and amethyst. Like Libra, ametrine is great for balance, especially when it comes to emotions. Unlike Libra, it can help make decisions and help you be willing to take action. Libra will like this unique crystal for its ability to end conflict, overcome change, and boost compatibility. Keep a piece of ametrine in your hand when weighing an important decision.

PINK TOURMALINE: Even the flirtatious Libra can get their hearts broken every now and again. When that happens, Libra placements should pick up some pink tourmaline to nurse and heal their wounded hearts. Representing a love for humanity, pink tourmaline can help heal your heart and enhance your perception while restoring harmony to your life. Place a piece of pink tourmaline at your altar for self-love and healing.

SAPPHIRE: As one of the birthstones associated with Libra, sapphire is the stone of wisdom, encouraging stimulating conversations and banishing unwanted thoughts. Sapphire is also the stone of property, bringing joy, happiness, and good fortune. Wear a pair of sapphire earrings to a party to have a fun and stimulating time.

Herbs for Libra

PASSIONFLOWER: Despite being named passionflower, this herb doesn't stir up strong emotions. As an air sign, Libra has a sharp mind that can often be overwhelmed. Passionflower may help you cope with stress by calming the mind, making passionflower an ideal remedy. Burn some passionflower incense after a long day to unwind.

ROOIBOS: Rooibos is often used as a tasty herbal tea that Libra placements will love for its reddish-pink color. Rooibos, known as "red brush" in South Africa, is a rejuvenating tea that can bring inner peace, energy, courage, strength, and determination. It's also known as a heart tonic, helping with healing and longevity. Drink some rooibos tea to help keep your strength and energy up.

VIOLET: A beautiful flower for a sign ruled by the goddess of beauty, violets aren't only just pretty to look at. They bring protection, inspiration, and wishes, making them the perfect flowers of Libra placements. Peaceful Libra will enjoy the harmony and faithfulness that the violet can bring to their lives. Steep some violets in lukewarm milk and use it to rinse your face for beauty and glamour (just don't drink this brew afterwards).

Best Type of Spells and Magic for Libra

Love spells, glamour magic, sigils, creative magic, coven forming, spells that promote fairness and karma

Ruled by Venus, the planet of art and beauty, Libras have an artistic nature about them that makes them very creative. Bring that artsy side to your spell work with this creative spell that encourages you to play and make magic.

MATERIALS

- Watercolor or acrylic paints (any color you feel like but do include white, blue, red, yellow, and green)
- Paintbrush
- Cup of water
- 1 blank canvas

1 Set the yellow, red, blue, green, and white paints in front of you. Wet the paintbrush, dab it into the yellow paint, and make a small brushstroke on the canvas while saying, "I call upon the element of air to make my image clear and true."

2 Clean the brush and repeat step 2 with the color red, saying, "I call upon the element of fire to let my ideas and passion burn brightly in my creative work."

3 Clean the brush and repeat step 2 with the color blue, saying, "I call upon the element of water to let my true emotions run deep through me and only the canvas."

4 Clean the brush and repeat step 2 with the color green, saying, "I call upon the element of earth to bring my visions into reality and ground me in my artistic practice."

5 When you are finished, cover your brushstrokes with white paint saying, "With this paint, I'm sealing the energy of the elements within."

6 Now start painting! You can paint whatever you like. If you are trying to manifest something, paint it. If you are using sigil magic, paint the sigil. Or, just let yourself go wild and paint abstract art, letting the colors and vibrations guide you. You don't need to be a skilled artist. Just imagine with each stroke of paint that you are channeling your magic from the brush to the page.

7 When you are done, sign your name on the bottom, sealing it. As you sign, say, "With my signature, so mote it be."

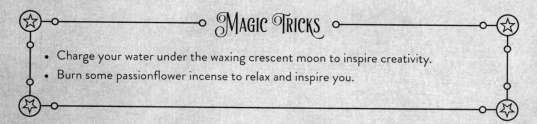

Magic Tricks

- Charge your water under the waxing crescent moon to inspire creativity.
- Burn some passionflower incense to relax and inspire you.

Scorpio

MAGNETIC * DRIVEN * POWERFUL

SEASON: October 23–November 21
GLYPH: ♏
SYMBOL: The Scorpion
ELEMENT: Water
MODALITY: Fixed
PLANET: Mars
HOUSE: 8th House
BODY PARTS: The reproductive system
COLORS: Black, red, brown
WHEEL OF THE YEAR: Samhain

Scorpio is the ultimate witch: blessed with a mysterious aura, a cunning mind, and the kind of natural intensity that both seduces and frightens. Scorpio is not afraid to walk on the darker side of life, as that's where the truth of life is hidden, and that secret truth equals power. Scorpio is always playing the long game so they can achieve what they desire. Their power lies in their ability to go deeper, plot harder, and focus their power with accurate precision.

Scorpio does not act on impulse; they carefully make a decision and then lie in wait for the perfect moment to strike. Do not mess with a Scorpio; they do not forgive easily and return each slight threefold. They love deeply, but they hold grudges like lovers.

On the wheel of the year, the Sabbat holiday, Samhain, is held on October 31, right in the middle of Scorpio season. During Samhain, the veil between the human and the spirit realms is at its thinnest, so we celebrate by honoring the dead, celebrating life, and preparing for the end of the harvest season. Scorpio embraces transformation: birth to adulthood, life to death, poverty to riches. Scorpio understands the cycles of life: when one journey ends, another one soon begins—that is the power of infinity.

Scorpio in the Natal Chart

If you have Scorpio in your big three, your inner witch may be stronger in different areas: you may look like a witch in Scorpio rising, or you may cast spells using raw emotions with a Scorpio moon. Here's how your Scorpio energy manifests itself.

Scorpio Sun

A Scorpio sun's life purpose is to go deep into the shadows—to the darkest part of humanity, of our nature—to get to the truth. A Scorpio sun is famous for their intensity, their passion, and their inability to be swayed by anything other than their firmly held convictions that guide them through life. They do not shy away from the messy, gory, chaotic parts of life; in fact, they are drawn to them. Their true power comes from their ability to endure the worst of life's struggles and survive.

This all sounds pretty dramatic, but a Scorpio thrives off of the drama of life. They are also interested in what happens when life is over. They are not afraid to go in deep and wade through the depths of all that came before us and what will come after us. Though possessive, manipulative, scheming, and intense to the point of being destructive, at their best, a Scorpio sun is protective, powerful, clever, and ambitious.

If you are a Scorpio sun, the lesson for your spiritual journey is to embrace the shadows of life without getting lost in the darkness.

Scorpio Moon

Feelings and emotions take on an intensity for a Scorpio moon. Every feeling is deep and extreme, motivating all their actions, from love to revenge. Pain becomes purpose and love becomes devotion. A Scorpio moon does nothing halfway; their all or nothing mindset can be their greatest asset but also the cause of their undoing, which is why they conceal their emotions. Despite the intensity, a Scorpio moon does not wallow in their feelings like other signs. Instead, they use their emotions to transform themselves. They have seen abuse, misfortune, and darkness and come out the other side as a champion.

At their best, a Scorpio moon witch is determined in their craft, thinking deeply about their beliefs and how they can use their magic to manifest their creations. However, they can also be withholding with their magic and can be obsessed with their craft and resentful of other witches.

Scorpio Rising

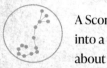 A Scorpio ascendant has a powerful aura felt by everyone as soon as they walk into a room. Even the most unassuming-looking Scorpio rising has an edge about them that people are either attracted to or disturbed by–even if they can't put their finger on the reason why. A Scorpio rising wants to be known for their ability to rise out of the ashes and transform into something rare and powerful. Never count a Scorpio rising out. Even when they are at their lowest point, at any moment they will make their big move and come back on top, stronger than ever. Their resilience is unmatched when it comes to getting what they want–even if it destroys them.

Scorpio ascendant first appears to be intense, brooding, and makes a strong impression with its uncanny magnetism. If you can get them to put their guard down, you'll find them to be patient, perceptive, and emotionally strong. A Scorpio ascendant looks like a witch, finding themselves casting spells, performing rituals, and casting a few hexes at their enemies.

Scorpio and Magic

Scorpio placements can manifest their magic in almost everything that they do, from making an altar devoted to their craft to cursing everyone who has wronged them. However, Scorpio's magic isn't all about settling scores—they also use their magic to tap into their highest powers. Here are the crystals, herbs, and rituals to help with that.

Crystals for Scorpio

 **LABRADORITE:** As the stone of transformation, labradorite is a soothing stone that can be used to ward off negativity energy and change the vibrations from bad to good. Like Scorpio, labradorite is a truth-seeker, able to get to the heart of any and all issues to discover the hidden depths of the subconscious. Wear a labradorite necklace when you are looking for the truth in the situation.

 **SODALITE:** As the harmonizing stone, sodalite provides calming energy when a Scorpio placement gets too wrapped up in their plans for world domination. While it eases the mind, it can also help unlock the sacred laws of the universe, something that Scorpio is always striving to solve. Meditate with a piece of sodalite when you're worried about getting grounded.

 **YELLOW TOPAZ:** One of the birthstones associated with Scorpio, yellow topaz is the manifesting stone, encouraging us to turn our goals into reality. Scorpio is always in the middle of a transformation and yellow topaz can help with clarity and encourage us to reach our highest potential. Wear a yellow topaz bracelet when you need a boost of confidence.

Herbs for Scorpio

BASIL: According to European folklore, basil belonged to Satan, and one had to curse the ground as you planted it in order for it to grow properly. While that may not be true, it is the kind of reputation a Scorpio would appreciate. Basil can help focus the mind and bring love, happiness, and money into your life. Carry a basil leaf in your wallet or purse to attract money.

CORIANDER: Scorpios are both secretive and truth seeking, so they are naturally drawn to the magical coriander herb that is used both for divination and for keeping secrets. Scorpio placements will love the spice for its magical properties, including clairvoyance, prosperity, passion, and memory retention. Burn some coriander to bring some passion into your life (especially in the bedroom).

WORMWOOD: Don't let the name fool you; there are no worms on this plant. Instead, wormwood is a powerful herb that can connect us with the spiritual realm. Scorpio placements can use wormwood to commune with the dead and increase their psychic ability and protection. Place wormwood flowers and leaves in a sachet for protection against accidents.

Best Type of Spells and Magic for Scorpio

Divination, clairvoyance, past life readings, herbalism, potion crafting, banishment spells, shadow work, luck spells, sex magic

A SPELL FOR SCORPIO

All Scorpio placements never forget and never forgive; it's part of the reason they can be so terrifying. However, Scorpios would be much happier and be able to focus on their goals (like world domination) if they could learn to let some things go. Here is a spell to move on and create your own closure.

MATERIALS

- A quiet place where you will not be disturbed
- White piece of paper
- Black marker (banishing negativity, letting go)
- Bowl of fresh water charged by the waning gibbous moon

Magic Trick

Light some white candles after you destroy the paper to bring peace into your life.

1 On the piece of paper, write the situation that you've been holding onto. Get into details. How does it make you feel? You can get creative, including drawing, creating a sigil, or even stabbing the page. Go wild.

2 When you have it all out there, fold the paper in half. Then fold it again, and again. Each time you fold, imagine the situation getting smaller and smaller in your life, no longer taking up so much space.

3 When you fold the paper up as small as you can, hold it upon the water and say, "I take this anger, the sorrow, this pain, and I let it go. I send you back to the place from whence you came. Your trouble won't trouble me. For my highest good, so mote it be."

4 Submerge the paper into the water, soaking it completely; watch the ink from the marker bleed through. When the paper is so wet it can no longer be read, pour the water out and throw the paper away. Now you can move on.

SAGITTARIUS

HONEST ✳ OPTIMISTIC ✳ ADVENTUROUS

SEASON: November 22–December 21
GLYPH: ♐
SYMBOL: The Archer
ELEMENT: Fire
MODALITY: Mutable
PLANET: Jupiter
HOUSE: 9th House
BODY PARTS: Thighs, hips, liver, pituitary glands
COLORS: Crimson, plum, royal blue
WHEEL OF THE YEAR: Transition from autumn into winter

Sagittarius is a sign that is in a constant state of reinvention. They are always on the go, bouncing from one location, one job, one project to the next, driven by their need for freedom and change. However, it isn't because Sagittarius is flighty or indecisive; they are simply expanding their horizons as well as themselves, creating new personas: the sage, the adventurer, the missionary, the free spirit, the witch, the traveler, the risk taker.

Next to their love of change and motion, Sagittarius's most recognizable trait is their optimism. A Sagittarius can take bold risks and change their lives on a whim because of their belief that everything will eventually work out. You couldn't quit your day job and move to Bali if you were a natural pessimist, could you? A Sagittarius takes these wild leaps of faith because that is the truest way to learn something in this life. By pulling back their arrow towards a new horizon, they are making their world a little more interesting.

Sagittarius season marks the transition from autumn into winter. We gather the last of the harvest and prepare for the long winter ahead. Sagittarius embraces the ending of the season, excited for the new cycle ahead.

Sagittarius in the Natal Chart

If you have Sagittarius in your big three, you may study Wicca through reading books (like this one) or traveling around to visit covens, attend conferences, or stop at spiritual places. When you expand your mind, you expand your magic. Here's how your Sagittarius energy manifests itself in different placements.

Sagittarius Sun

A Sagittarius sun's life purpose is to experience all that life has to offer. They are here to expand their intellectual horizons and see everything that there is to see—and try doing it all at once. A typical Sagittarius sun tries to fill three lifetimes' worth of experience into their time on earth. They learn by doing and often jump headfirst into whatever draws their interest and stimulates their mind.

A Sagittarius sun has an abundance of faith to keep them going. In most situations, they think with their gut and act on instinct, and it's usually correct. Cheerful, philosophical, and honest, you'll usually run into these people while they're moving from one place to another as they can never stay still for long enough. However, this restlessness can make them irresponsible, impatient, and quick-tempered.

If you're a Sagittarius sun, the lesson for your spiritual practice is to embrace the changes that magic and Wicca can bring you while staying in your own lane.

Sagittarius Moon

A person with a Sagittarius moon has the heart of an adventurer, always longing to roam. Naturally happy-go-lucky, all a Sagittarius moon needs in life is the freedom to be able to go where they please. They need plenty of space to feel safe and cannot stand feeling caged in. If they feel they are limited or stuck in a boring routine, they are looking for an escape route. A Sagittarius moon needs excitement: meeting new people, learning new facts, having the next experience. Not only because it stimulates them, but because they can take what they learn and teach it to someone else, continuing the cycle of education. A Sagittarius moon is both the student and the teacher.

At their best, a Sagittarius moon witch is knowledgeable about all aspects of Wicca but open-minded about new practices, trying each new spell with optimism and exuberance. However, they can be impulsive with their magic, careless, and overconfident when casting.

Sagittarius Rising

Sagittarius ascendants are marked by their natural enthusiasm that is palpable to everyone who meets them. They are just so excited to share what they have been researching, the trip that they just took, or a new song they just discovered with you. In fact, they often speak as if they are an excitable professor giving a new lecture to an engaged classroom. Speaking with the confidence that only comes from experience, yet still energized, Sagittarius rising has a lot to give; but sometimes their passionate nature can rub people the wrong way, especially when they speak without thinking (which they do often). Their quick temper can easily land them in hot water, but they can usually smooth their way out of things by simply moving on. Blessed by their ruling planet, Jupiter, the planet of luck, Sagittarius risings will always land on their feet.

When you first meet a Sagittarius ascendant, they appear to be charming and knowledgeable, but flighty and thoughtless. However, once you get to know them, you'll discover that they are warm, fun loving, and wickedly funny. A Sagittarius rising can give sage wisdom about Wicca, helping people with their own relationship with their craft.

SAGITTARIUS AND MAGIC

Sagittarius placements can manifest their magic by expanding their mind and worldview. They are open to any type of magic and are willing to try anything once. Here are some crystals, herbs, and rituals to try to stay connected to your inner magic.

CRYSTAL FOR SAGITTARIUS

BLUE TOPAZ: When the fire sign burns too hot, it needs something cool to tame those flames. Blue topaz is associated with peace and tranquility, being able to calm things down before they blow up. Known for its ability to communicate clearly with self-assurance, blue topaz can help impulsive Sagittarius think before they speak. Wear a blue topaz necklace when having a big group meeting, so you choose your words carefully.

GREEN AVENTURINE: A crystal perfect for the adventuring sign, like Sagittarius, green aventurine promotes optimism, expanded viewpoints, and generosity. It helps keep the archer's heart open as it goes through life. Keep a piece of green aventurine by your desk as a reminder to keep your heart and mind open.

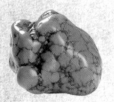

TURQUOISE: A stone for safe travels, turquoise is the perfect stone for Sagittarius to take on their travels through life. Turquoise brings tranquility, creativity, and financial blessings—all things Sagittarius needs to keep on moving in this life. Keep a piece of turquoise on you for safe travels.

Herbs for Sagittarius

CARNATION: As the sacred flower of Diana, the Roman goddess of the hunt, carnation is often used in protection and healing spells, though Sagittarius placements will also be drawn to the flower for its ability to bring personal courage, strength, virtue, and nobility. Hang some dried carnation buds over your doorway for protection.

DANDELION: Much like Sagittarius, dandelions grow deep yet go wherever the wind takes them. Dandelions represent the cycles of life, from birth to death to rebirth again. Sagittarius placements are drawn to dandelions for their strength, joy, intelligence, freedom, and longevity. Brew some dandelion tea to help boost your mental strength and increase your intuition.

RED CLOVER: Sagittarius is ruled by Jupiter, the planet of luck, and there's nothing luckier than a clover. While not the traditional four-leaf clover, red clovers add a touch of fiery passion to the lucky plant. Red clover also promotes self-actualization, spiritual purification, and increasing inner strength. It can also help Sagittarius placements become better listeners. Put some red clover in your bath to bring prosperity and financial gains.

Best Type of Spells and Magic for Sagittarius

Studying rituals, protection spells for safe travels, candle magic, artistic magic, study spells, sigils, covens

While a Sagittarius is blessed with luck and good fortune wherever they go, it's a good idea to have a spell they can take with them. This is a handy spell jar that Sagittarius can wear as a necklace or keychain, so they'll always have good fortune with them.

MATERIALS

- Small funnel or tweezers
- Small cork-topped glass jar or vial (it should have a loop on top to attach onto a necklace or keyring)
- Pinch of green aventurine chips (for optimism and luck)
- Pinch of turquoise chips (for safe travels and blessing)
- Pinch of pink Himalayan salt (for protection)
- Pinch of dried carnation (for courage and strength)
- Pinch of dried dandelion (for safe travel and wishes)
- Cord or keyring

1 Using the funnel or tweezers, place the ingredients, one layer at a time, into the jar or vial: the crystals, the salt, the herbs. Remember to thank each of your ingredients as you add them.

2 Before you cork the jar, hold it out in front of you and say, "With this jar, my spell is always with me. I am protected on my journey through life and blessed with the best intentions. So mote it be."

3 Attach the jar to a cord or keyring and take it with you.

Magic Tricks

- For an extra boost, write a sigil of your intention on a small piece of paper and place it in the spell jar.
- Seal your spell jar by melting candle wax onto the top of the jar. Use yellow wax for safe travel and positivity, or black wax for wisdom and protection.

Capricorn

AMBITIOUS * DEPENDABLE * PERSISTENT

SEASON: December 22–January 19
GLYPH: ♑
SYMBOL: The Sea-Goat
ELEMENT: Earth
MODALITY: Cardinal
PLANET: Saturn
HOUSE: 10th House
BODY PARTS: Knees, joints, skeletal system, teeth
COLORS: Gray, brown, black
WHEEL OF THE YEAR: Yule (the Winter Solstice)

Often considered a stern and serious sign, Capricorns appear and act older than they are. Their practical minds cut straight to the point, and their ambitious nature allows them to achieve great things so early in life that many assume they must be older. However, don't mistake a Capricorn's exterior for someone stuffy. Capricorns often have a wry sense of humor, and their deadpan delivery charms friends, lovers, and business associates alike. Capricorns know that nothing in this life comes easy, so they must enjoy it while they can.

Capricorn season begins with Yule, the Wiccan holiday to celebrate the winter solstice and the rebirth of the Great Horned God, which carries souls to the underworld. If you're used to seeing Capricorn symbolized by the goat, know that it's actually represented by the mythical sea-goat, an aquatic creature who is half-fish and half-goat. This perfectly symbolizes Capricorn: it can move easily in the water, but it can climb to the top of a mountain.

The winter solstice is the shortest day of the year, adding to Capricorn's brooding, pessimistic, and shy personality. However, after the darkest day of the year, each day gets a little brighter. Capricorn starts in darkness and slowly works its way into the light.

Capricorn in the Natal Chart

If you have Capricorn in your big three, you see magic as a means to an end, something that can help you achieve your ambitions. Coven meetings may be networking events as you try to use your craft to become powerful. Remember, this is a spiritual journey as well. Here's how Capricorn energy manifests itself in different placements.

Capricorn Sun

A Capricorn sun's life purpose is to always be striving towards a goal, as you are fulfilled by worthwhile achievements. Traditionally, people think this goal is money or career success, but this isn't always the case. Capricorns can be driven by the pursuit of knowledge, praise, helping others, justice, or the desire to create. Whatever Capricorn sun chooses to do with their life, they want to be the best, giving them a reputation of being a high achiever.

Gifted with practicality, diligence, and a creative mind, Capricorns are skilled problem solvers, creating solutions out of thin air. They can make any situation work—and work to their advantage. Though Capricorns can be controlling, rigid, skeptical, and harsh, they do have a strict moral code that guides them through life. At their best, Capricorn sun is ambitious, mature, independent, and determined.

If you are a Capricorn sun, the lesson for your spiritual practice is to let go of your fear of failure. You are too strong of a witch to fail, so believe in yourself.

Capricorn Moon

If you asked a Capricorn moon about feelings or their emotions, they might dryly reply, "Feelings? What feelings? I'm dead inside," with a sly half-smile. It's true that Capricorn moons are emotionally self-reliant, preferring to keep their emotions to themselves instead of giving even a glimpse of what's going on below the surface. They feel safe when they are in control of a situation and try to solve their own problems. They feel best when they're accomplishing tasks, being productive, and proving their use to others. Overwhelmed with feelings of responsibility, they would rather ignore their own emotions and take care of others. This could lead them to struggle to make connections—both with others and their bodies. Capricorn moons need to learn to take care of themselves instead of working themselves to exhaustion.

At their best, the Capricorn moon witch is dedicated to their craft, as their energy is steadfast, and patient with ambitious spells. However, they might not always believe in their craft and can have trouble bonding with a coven, preferring a solo practice, which can be isolating.

Capricorn Rising

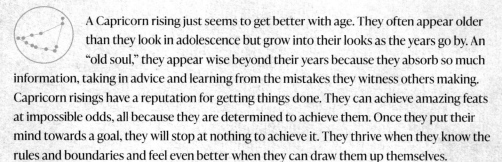 A Capricorn rising just seems to get better with age. They often appear older than they look in adolescence but grow into their looks as the years go by. An "old soul," they appear wise beyond their years because they absorb so much information, taking in advice and learning from the mistakes they witness others making. Capricorn risings have a reputation for getting things done. They can achieve amazing feats at impossible odds, all because they are determined to achieve them. Once they put their mind towards a goal, they will stop at nothing to achieve it. They thrive when they know the rules and boundaries and feel even better when they can draw them up themselves.

Capricorn ascendants first appear to be quiet, stern, and reserved, but if you're lucky enough to have a Capricorn rising open up to you, you'll see the pure power of their personality: coming off as charming, witty, and expressive. A Capricorn rising witch is often seen working alone, guarding their magic with care.

Capricorn and Magic

Capricorn placements can manifest their magic in the start of winter, using the heat of their own magic to warm them. While they don't need much to create powerful magic, here are some crystals, herbs, and rituals to enchant the process.

Crystals for Capricorn

GARNET: The birthstone of Capricorn, garnet reenergizes the body and soul, bringing balance to both. Garnet gives Capricorn placements passion, courage, success, and the hope that they need to tackle their goals while giving them an extra boost of self-confidence. It also gives extra sensuality and sex drive to bring some more pleasure to the sea-goat. Wear a garnet ring or bracelet when you're about to do something brave.

SMOKY QUARTZ: This is a great grounding crystal to help you get focused when you are feeling like your ambitions are spinning out of control or you just need a little motivation to get started. This stabilizing crystal also protects Capricorns from negative thoughts and energies. Put a piece of smoky quartz on your desk for motivation and protection.

OBSIDIAN: This piece of volcanic glass holds great healing power within. A grounding stone, obsidian can help Capricorn heal the mind, body, and soul. It can also help Capricorn cut through the fiction and get to the truth of any issue—from the lies people tell you to the core of your inner demons. Keep a piece of obsidian at your altar for honesty.

Herbs for Capricorn

ROSEMARY: This common kitchen herb isn't just for dinner anymore. Rosemary may improve mood, brain health, and memory. Magically, rosemary is used for healing, love, preventing nightmares, and protection. It's used as decoration for Yule, along with holly and mistletoe. Add a handful of fresh rosemary leaves to your bath to make you more memorable to everyone you meet.

SHEPHERD'S PURSE: Part of the mustard family, shepherd's purse gets its name from its heart-shaped leaves that look like the purses that shepherds used. Magically, shepherd's purse is used for protection, prosperity, emotional strength, willpower, and self-esteem. Put some shepherd's purse in a satchel and carry it with you for prosperity.

THYME: Another common kitchen staple, this culinary herb may be good for lowering Capricorn's high blood pressure and boosting their immunity during the cold months. Magically, thyme is used for health, healing, courage, strength, and love. Burn a sprig of thyme when you need a boost of courage; use it as an ingredient in your meal before you do something important.

Best Type of Spells and Magic for Capricorn

Abundance spells, manifestation charms, healing spells, garden magic, herbalism, job spells, grounding rituals, a home blessing

Here is a handy spell that can benefit all Capricorn placements. It is an abundance spell to help see your goals grow until they come to life. For what started as a seed can grow into your wildest dreams, with some effort and hard work.

MATERIALS

- Pen (preferably with green ink)
- Small piece of paper
- Small pot
- Soil
- Rosemary seeds
- Water

1 In a quiet place, free of all distractions, write down all the goals you wish to accomplish within the next six months to a year. Write down everything you truly want. (Keep your writing small.)

2 When you finish your list, write, "I will accomplish all of this for my highest good. Everything I need to achieve is already with me, so mote it be," before signing and dating it.

3 Fold the paper up as small as it can go, preferably the size of a nickel.

4 Fill the pot with soil and plant the rosemary seeds.

5 Toward the edge of the pot, away from the rosemary seeds, plant your list under the soil.

6 As you get ready to water the soil, say, "With this water, I'm bringing life to what I want. I'm ready to achieve my wildest dreams. For my highest good, so mote it be." Water the soil.

7 Continue to tend to and care for your rosemary plant. As it grows, imagine that it is you, growing and moving into achieving your goals.

Magic Tricks

- If you have the space, get a potted elm, fir, or pine tree or sapling and do the same thing but for longer goals (10+ years), as those trees are associated with Capricorn.
- Create an alter around your plant, surrounding it with Capricorn's crystals, photos of what you want to achieve, etc.
- For best results, do this on a Saturday, as it is the day associated with Capricorn.

AQUARIUS

ORIGINAL ✳ INNOVATIVE ✳ SOCIALLY CONSCIOUS

SEASON: January 20–February 18
GLYPH: ♒
SYMBOL: The Water-bearer
ELEMENT: Air
MODALITY: Fixed
PLANET: Saturn
HOUSE: 11th House
BODY PARTS: Ankles, calves, shins, the circulatory system
COLORS: Electric blue, white, violet
WHEEL OF THE YEAR: Imbolc

Aquarius is the sign of contradictions. Its name is Aquarius and its symbol is the water-bearer, but its ruling sign is air. They have a deep love of humanity but are often considered to be loners. They are a fixed sign that is naturally reluctant to change, but Aquarians are our innovators, questioning existing structures and imagining what would happen if we did things differently. Aquarians embrace the weirdness of life and ask: "What could we do if we broke all the rules that limit us? What could we become?"

Aquarians are weird, a description they wear with honor. They are not the people who color inside the lines; they make art. They are the outsiders who look and wonder: Why do we live like that? They have the courage to ask questions, and dare us to do and achieve what is different, because the only freedom we have is a world without limitations.

On the Wheel of the Year, the Wicca Sabbat, Imbolc, falls in the middle of Aquarius season, on February 1. It is the last Sabbat and last holiday before the new year begins, and it serves as a celebration of life starting to wake up after a long winter. This is a time of creativity, letting go of the past, and making room for new life—everything Aquarius believes in.

Aquarius in the Natal Chart

If you have Aquarius in your big three, you have a unique and innovative way of approaching your craft. You like to experiment and try new things—even if they blow up in your face. Here is how your Aquarius energy manifests itself in different placements.

Aquarius Sun

An Aquarius sun's life purpose is to forge a new path in life. They see the way old and outdated systems have failed us in the past and strive to put their energy, intelligence, and magic towards creating new solutions to life's problems that work best for everyone. Craving intellectual stimulation, they yearn for a problem they can untangle, a theory they can try to unravel, and a trail of clues to follow to discover something new. They love humanity on an impersonal level, wanting to help people without the emotional entanglements.

Gifted with a keen mind, a unique worldview, and an idealistic heart, an Aquarius sun lets their freak flag fly as they are free from the social norms that are forced upon society. However, despite their openness to change, they can be quite stubborn; their intellect makes them aloof, often lost in their own heads. However, it's their quirky nature that makes them stand out in the zodiac.

If you are an Aquarius sun, the lesson for your spiritual practice is to be present in the physical world as you use your magic for real-world applications.

Aquarius Moon

From an early age, Aquarius moons have always felt they were "different" from other people. This may be because of their keen observational abilities that allows them to watch others and make comparisons. However, as they quickly learn, being different isn't a bad thing. The sooner an Aquarius moon is free of the oppressive box that society has put them in, the happier they will be. However, they will still always be loners at their core, watching people but never quite feeling like they are part of the group. Aquarius moon needs its space to feel emotionally secure, but it needs to feel understood to feel safe. That is the conflicting desire that lies in the heart of this moon.

At their best, the Aquarius moon witch is progressive when it comes to Wicca traditions, willing to switch things up. They also create unique spells and stick to their ideals when crafting. However, they are often aloof in coven meetings (though they invited everyone), and don't use emotions in crafting.

Aquarius Rising

 You'll notice an Aquarius ascendant very quickly as they are so... *different* from everyone else in the room, either by their mannerisms, their style, or their overall aura. Aquarius risings are even different from one another; just like snowflakes, no two are exactly alike. An Aquarius rising enjoys being different from the crowd, and they want to be known for their abilities to do things differently. That they are the innovators that change the game for everyone. Their humanitarianism easily comes to the surface when volunteering at shelters, going to protests, or speaking up at city council meetings. They are made to shake things up—for better or for worse.

At first glance, an Aquarius rising appears to be individualistic, highly intelligent, but a little standoffish and shocking. However, once you get to know them, you'll discover that they are altruistic, original, and accepting of others. You'll see an Aquarius rising forming a coven to create a magical community but usually hanging low during the actual meetings.

Aquarius and Magic

Aquarius placements use magic in unique ways that make traditional witches give them a double take. We aren't asking you to "conform" to the Wiccan norm, but these crystals, herbs, and rituals can give you a boost.

Crystals for Aquarius

CLEAR QUARTZ: As the master healer, clear quartz is the most versatile crystal as it draws its strength from the power of the crystals around it, just like Aquarius knows that we are better as a collective. Clear quartz can help Aquarius placements reach their true potential, gain abundance, and bring out their best intentions to help the world. Put clear quartz near other crystals at your altar to amplify their energy.

FLUORITE: For the disorganized Aquarius placement, fluorite is all about balancing things out so you can focus on the goals and issues that really matter. Fluorite can help improve communication skills, dispel negative energy, and help the airy Aquarius stay grounded on their journey. Write your goals on a piece of paper and place a piece of fluorite on it to help them manifest.

HEMATITE: A strong grounding stone, hematite is here to protect Aquarius from any negative energy that may come their way. Hematite is used as a barrier so that Aquarius can continue the important work they need to be doing without interference. Keep a piece of hematite by your front door to protect you from negativity.

Herbs for Aquarius

CACAO: Not your typical herb, but Aquarius isn't your typical sign either. Cacao beans come from the cacao tree and are used to make chocolate and cocoa butter. Cacao brings grounding energy, prosperity, and clarity when it comes to purpose, love, and personal growth. It can also help heal the energy within the body. Perform a cacao ceremony by gathering people together to drink cocoa while having inspired discussions.

FENNEL: A supermarket favorite, fennel is a perfect addition to spells for its courage, strength, protection, love, and divination properties. (It's also quite delicious, and its tea has been used for soothing aching tummies.) Make some fennel soup while studying for a test to improve memory and retain the information.

STAR ANISE: A magically shaped herb for a unique sign, star anise is great for increasing your psychic awareness and divination practices. It is also good for cleansing energy and as protection against not-so-friendly ghosts. Tie a string around a piece of star anise to use as a pendulum.

Best Type of Spells and Magic for Aquarius

Coven magic, manifesting for social change, protest magic, innovation spells, using poetry as spells, signals, new project spells, techno-magic

As the astrological sign associated with innovation and technology, Aquarius placements look toward modern ways to bring witchcraft into their lives. Here's a simple spell that brings spell casting into the modern age.

MATERIALS

- Your cell phone

Magic Trick

Place a piece of clear quartz on top of your phone before casting to clear the energy.

1 Cast your circle and take a few deep breaths to center yourself.

2 When you're ready, take out your phone. Open up an instant messenger app, other social media app, or your email.

3 Think about the spell you want to cast. What are you hoping to bring to you? Success? Clarity? New opportunities? Think very clearly about the spell you wish to cast.

4 Pull up your emoji keyboard and carefully pick out the emojis that best represent what you want your spell to bring you. Don't overthink this; just use your intuition. Pick at least five.

5 Once your intention is set and your emojis haveen been chosen, cast it by sending it. You can send this emoji spell to your coven, post on your social media page, or just email it to yourself. Unleash it to the universe!

Pisces

IMAGINATIVE ✳ COMPASSIONATE ✳ PERCEPTIVE

SEASON: February 19–March 20
GLYPH: ♓
SYMBOL: The Fishes
ELEMENT: Water
MODALITY: Mutable
PLANET: Jupiter
HOUSE: 12th House
BODY PARTS: Feet, toes, lymphatic system
COLORS: Seafoam green, lilac, silver
WHEEL OF THE YEAR: Transition from winter into spring

At the end of the zodiac wheel, Pisces is not only a representation of an ending, but the wisdom we have gained at the end of our journey. Pisces contains a little of each sign within their personality. This makes them feel emotions much deeper than others. However, unlike fellow water signs, a Pisces does not feel the need to hide those emotions. Rather, they feel it is their responsibility to share the gifts of love and other emotions with the world.

Pisces are incredibly adaptable to getting along with people of all walks of life. Highly intuitive, sensitive, and perceptive, they often give off the same energy that is given to them. If you act aggressively towards them, they will come at you with aggression. If you come at them with kindness, they will do the same. That's why it can be so hard to understand a Pisces, though they are longing to understand and be understood.

Pisces season comes at the end of winter as we prepare for the spring. While everything is still hibernating, we get to see that glimmer of hope that spring will soon be here. Pisces lives in that glimmer of hope. Even though we are at the end of a journey, a new one is just around the corner.

Pisces in the Natal Chart

If you have Pisces in your big three, you are highly intuitive, and that intuition guides most of your craft. You are usually the first with the tarot cards, or at least curious about the spiritual and fortune-telling side of Wicca and witchcraft. Here's how your Pisces energy manifests in different placements.

Pisces Sun

 A Pisces sun's life purpose is to leave this world better than they found it. This may seem like a big ask for a mere mortal to complete, but a Pisces sun is always on a higher level than those around them. Intuitive, compassionate, and a natural healer, a Pisces sun takes their personality from many resources, but their goal is simple: to make a positive difference. From spreading love to their community to taking care of friends when they need them most, a Pisces sun will be defined by the love they give.

A Pisces sun has an elusive quality that makes it challenging for people to get to know them intimately, though people seem to open up to them with ease. Much like water, they reflect the energy others give to them, but their emotions run deep. They best express themselves through creative projects that helps them channel all those big feelings they have been holding onto.

If you are a Pisces sun, the lesson for your spiritual practice is to put up emotional and psychic boundaries so you don't absorb negative vibrations.

Pisces Moon

 A person with a Pisces moon is a dreamer, someone who is often lost in fantasies and forgetting to come back down to earth. However, a Pisces moon needs their dreams, their creative outlets and their expansive imagination to feel safe and secure. Pisces moons are sensitive souls who can easily feel the pain of others as if it were happening them personally. Because they can get lost in the suffering, they need a way to escape, especially when their emotional battery is low. Guided by their intuition, a Pisces moon is gifted with a sixth sense. They know when the vibes are off or when something is wrong. From a feeling they get in the pit of their stomach to hearing a slight sharpness in someone's voice, they'll know.

At their best, Pisces moon witches are loyal to their coven, practice magic and rituals with gentle love, and are an inspiration to their fellow witches. However, they can be absent-minded when it comes to spell work, and they can be gullible to less-than-friendly people pretending to be Wiccans. When hurt, they can play the martyr.

Pisces Rising

 A first impression of a Pisces ascendant may not always be a good one, mainly because they're usually spacing out, lost in the fantasy world they create in their minds when the physical one gets too boring or too sad. However, moving past the absent-minded first impression, a Pisces rising has a gentleness about them that people pick up on instantly, a sweet tenderness written on their face that can melt even the most stoic character. There is something about them that makes it easy to open to them, even if they are a stranger. However, being the sounding board to other people's problems makes them feel misunderstood and lonely. They can go from lively to moody in a matter of seconds, just because the vibes of the room changed a little. So if you see them staring off into space, just give it a minute, they'll be right back.

Pisces ascendant first appears to be spacey, disorganized, mysterious, but very sweet. However, once you get to know them, you'll discover how creative, warm, sentimental, and complex they can be. They are gentle witches, tending to their coven with love, care, and a soothing aura that can calm even the most passionate coven.

Pisces and Magic

Pisces placements are very connected to their magic when they are connected to their emotions, when they put their feelings center stage and use them as a guiding force. This is especially true when seeing the future or manifesting comfort. Here are some crystals, herbs, and rituals to best tap into your power.

Crystals for Pisces

 **AMETHYST:** One of the birthstones associated with Pisces, amethyst is a spiritual crystal that allows the deep Pisces to get in touch with the spiritual world with ease. Amethyst also has the power to calm down the emotional water sign while increasing their already high intuition. Wear an amethyst necklace while meditating to calm down.

 **BLACK TOURMALINE:** Widely used as a talisman in ancient cultures to ward off demons, black tourmaline absorbs all negativity, including emotions. It can help protect empathic Pisces placements from energy vampires. Wear a black tourmaline bracelet to absorb the negative emotions around you.

 **CALCITE:** Calcite brings soothing energy to the often emotionally sensitive Pisces and gives them the balance they need to stay grounded. The stone also provides emotional and mental clarity, helping Pisces placements make decisions, inspire their creativity, and help them reach enlightenment. Hold calcite in your hand when you need to make a major decision.

Herbs for Pisces

LILAC: A beautiful flower for the gentle Pisces, lilac can really lighten the mood, which is especially useful for the emotional water sign. Lilac can also ward off and banish negative energy and draw positive energy in to bring pleasure, especially when it comes to romance. Spray some lilac mist in a room to lighten the mood.

MUGWORT: Often associated with divination and dreams, mugwort can help Pisces placements gain clairvoyance in their dreams and even see into the future. Mugwort is also an herb that can be used for protection, strength, and creativity. Add mugwort to tea before bed to have dreams of the future.

WITCH HAZEL: You've probably seen and used witch hazel oil in your skincare products, but its uses are more than skin deep. For centuries, witch hazels have been used to divine for water and other divination purposes. Pisces placements can use witch hazel for healing, cleansing, protection, and wisdom. Write your intentions on a piece of paper and place it in a bowl. Cover the paper with witch hazel and leave it in the light of a waning moon. The next morning, bury the witch hazel and paper away from your home for it to manifest.

Best Type of Spells and Magic for Aquarius

Divination, sea magic, past life exploration, dream magic, healing magic, sacred bath rituals, cycles of ending and rebirth, creative magic

Pisces placements are famous for having strong, vivid dreams. Sometimes these dreams can help you see into the future, often vivid, as if they were real. Help strengthen your sixth sense by taking a relaxing bath before bed to bring dreams of the future.

MATERIALS

- ½ cup Epsom salts (cleansing the energy)
- 6 drops witch hazel essential oil (for divination)
- 2 tablespoons dried mugwort (for psychic visions)
- 2 tablespoons dried lilac or 6 drops lilac essential oil (brings pleasure)
- Bowl
- Spoon
- Amethyst crystal (to get in touch with the spiritual world)
- Black tourmaline crystal (for protection)
- Notebook
- Pen

1 Mix the salt, essential oil, and dried herbs together in a bowl. As you stir, visualize your energy going into the mixture.

2 Draw yourself a hot bath before you go to bed. Cast a circle around you. Place the amethyst and black tourmaline on the side of the tub.

3 Pour the mixture into the water, saying, "With this mixture, I open myself up to whatever the future has in store for me. Bring me a glimpse of the future in my dreams. For my highest good, so mote it be."

4 Get in the tub and relax. Don't think too hard about anything, just soak it all in.

5 When you're finished, get ready for bed, keeping a notebook and pen by your bedside.

6 When you wake up, write down the dreams you had. See what comes up.

Magic Tricks

- Light some purple or white candles in the bathroom to call upon the spiritual energies and allow yourself to be open to psychic dreams.
- If you do not have a bathtub, put the ingredients in a sachet and hang it in the bathroom under the shower head as you take your shower. Or turn it into a scrub by adding a ½ cup of coconut oil to the mixture.
- For best results, do this under a full moon.

3
Understanding the Magic of the Moon

For centuries, the moon has been a source of inspiration, wonder, and even obsession. She is in our poetry and our art, worshipped in our deities, and is simply a calming presence while we gaze up at the night sky. Perhaps it's because she invokes a sense of mystery, as she often has a part of her appearance cloaked in shadow. Or is it because she has so much impact on our lives here on earth, from tracking the passage of time to the way she pulls the oceans' tides? Humans are made of up to sixty percent water, so it is no surprise that we are also pulled in by the moon's power. However, the moon's most significant influence lies within the flow of our own magic.

Like many other religions and spiritual practices, Wicca holds the moon in the highest esteem as she represents the cycles of life. Everything is born, goes through the phases of life, dies, and is reborn again. The moon and her cycle help us understand and embrace the natural rhythms of the earth as we connect to the mighty power of nature. Even the most powerful witch must recognize the influence of the moon and remain humble in her light. When we align ourselves with lunar energy, we can truly tap into our highest good.

Wiccans also associate the moon with mystery, passion, fertility, emotions, and our inner self. Here are just a couple of ways Wiccans use the moon in their practice.

The Triple Moon Goddess

One of the influential symbols in Wicca is the Triple Moon Goddess, also known simply as the Triple Goddess. You may recognize the Triple Moon Goddess by her symbol: a full moon between two crescent moons. This represents the three figures that the Triple Goddess embodies: the Maiden, the Mother, and the Crone. They represent the cycle of life, death, and never-ending circle of life.

THE MAIDEN: The Maiden represents the start of the journey that all witches must go through. It is the beginning stages of our lives where the world is full of untapped potential. The Maiden also represents the waxing phase of the moon, when we move towards becoming fulfilled. The Maiden is innocent but curious, encouraging us to strive for new experiences.

THE MOTHER: The Mother represents the middle of our journey through life. Representing the full moon, the Mother is us reaching our highest potential and creating something that will leave our mark on this world, creating our legacy. However, despite being called "the Mother," it does not always have to represent having children, fertility, or even parenthood. The Mother could also be giving birth to an idea, creating art, starting a business, or simply creating a life that one enjoys. The Mother encourages us to step into our full power with courage and intention.

THE CRONE: The Crone marks the ending of a cycle, where we've already reached our peak and are now slowly getting ready for our rebirth and renewal. The Crone represents the waning of the moon, a time for rest, reflection, and grounding. The Crone is not a sad period, as we have more wisdom, given to us by the best teachers of all: time and experience. We can shoulder more responsibility and lead the next generation using the skills we have earned. The Crone encourages us to embrace all our former selves, as they have led us here.

Esbats

In addition to the Wiccan Wheel of the Year that celebrates the four equinoxes and the four Sabbats, Wiccans also have a second wheel of the year that celebrates all twelve of the full moons throughout the year. These Esbats are ritual celebrations of the moon and her goddess as we honor her in her full glory.

Because the Triple Moon Goddess is so sacred to Wicca, covens typically come together to form various rituals around the moon, from performing group casting or charging their collective energy, to just basking in the moon's restorative light.

One ritual that covens perform during Esbat is the act of drawing down the moon. This is a transformative and spiritual process where the leader or priestess of the coven uses their energy to "pull down" the moon's energy into the physical body of the witches to capture the moon's power within them. The moon's full energy can help them increase their casting ability, help them manifest better, and even create healing energy within themselves.

Esbats can be done with a coven or held by individual witches. Some witches even hold Esbats for the new moon. Any method is perfectly acceptable, as long as you do what feels right to you and your relationship with the moon.

Every two and a half years, two full moons will happen within the same calendar month. The additional full moon is known as the blue moon, and it is a powerful full moon, giving off a higher energy frequency than the regular moon. When a blue moon happens, you must take full advantage of it—do not let this time go to waste as you create some serious magic.

The Lunar Phases

It takes twenty-seven to twenty-nine days for the moon to orbit the earth. Because the sun illuminates the moon, we often see the moon at different angles at a time: sometimes full, sometimes in a crescent shape, and sometimes we cannot see it at all. These appearances are known as phases. The moon goes through eight of them during its monthly cycle. Each of these eight phases has a unique vibration that it transmits to us on earth.

Witches often use the lunar phases to help plan out spells, rituals, and even hold coven meetings, like Esbats. By learning about the lunar phases, you can use the moon's energy in your craft, understand the vibes of the day, and even boost your spells.

The New Moon

The new moon represents the beginning of the new lunar cycle that is taking place. It represents a clean slate where you can reflect on the previous cycle and think about your dreams and goals for the upcoming phases. It is a time for setting intentions to manifest your desires. Try intention setting rituals, success spells, cleansing rituals, divination, manifesting, blessing, breaking curses, and emotional reflection.

Waxing Crescent Moon

Now that you know what you want, it is time to plan and prepare during the waxing crescent moon. Energy is absorbed easily during this phase as you strive to plant the seeds to manifest your goals. This is not the time to play coy; be loud with what you want. Try beauty spells, boosting psychic abilities, positivity spells, manifesting positive energy, and spell crafting.

Waxing Gibbous Moon

Now is the time to refine your techniques and rethink your strategies. You may realize that you have to try a different approach to get what you want or change your goals to make them more achievable. On the other hand, the waxing gibbous moon is also a sign that you are close to achieving what you desire. Just keep going! Try strength renewal rituals, energy boost spells, attraction spells, success spells, healing spells, and constructive magic.

First Quarter Moon

It is now time to take inspired action to get what you desire. As you move forward on your journey, you may start to face obstacles that are blocking you. During this phase, you need to show strength, determination, and commitment to overcome those obstacles. Try performing rituals, money spells, success spells, finding lost objects, spells for strength, attracting a familiar (animal companion), and protection spells.

Full Moon

The full moon is the most powerful of all the lunar phases. Harvest the fruits of your endeavors and complete the plans you made during the new moon. Use the raw power of the moon to bring your manifestations to life and develop your magical and spiritual selves. This is also when Esbats are typically held. Try making moon water, charging tools, meditation, divination, dreamwork, gratitude, letting go rituals, protection spells, healing spells, creativity spells, moon baths, job spells, money spells, love spells, beauty spells, and Esbat rituals.

Waning Gibbous Moon

After absorbing the power of the full moon, the waning gibbous moon encourages you to take a step back and practice introspection. It is a time for practicing gratitude and releasing what no longer serves you. Look at what you have gained during the full moon and how it makes you feel. Try cleansing negative energy, breaking curses, banishing spells, unbinding spells, practicing gratitude, and ending spells and rituals.

Last Quarter Moon

After all that introspection, the last quarter moon encourages you to let go of the unhealthy habits you have developed and find ways to overcome your obstacles. This is a period of transformation as you get ready for the end of this lunar cycle. Try transition rituals, breaking bad habits, cleansing, banishing, resisting temptations, and spells to overcome obstacles.

Waning Crescent Moon

As the last phase of the lunar cycle, it's time to rest and reflect. Surrender to the universe and let the Triple Goddess take the wheel. Rest your mind, body, and spirit so you can prepare for the new lunar cycle. Don't push yourself too hard right now; you'll need to save up your energy. Try banishing, relaxation rituals and spells, curses, cleansing, and silent reflection.

The Moon Through The Signs

It takes the moon twenty-eight and a half days to go through the twelve zodiac signs, so the moon stays in a certain sign for two and a half days. During that time, the moon takes on the characteristics of that sign and transfers those energy vibrations onto us on earth. Learning what sign the moon is in can help you understand the energy of the day, how to use that energy in your craft, and help you make the most of the lunar phase. It also helps you understand the themes of the new and full moon, where the influences of the zodiac signs are increased.

Aries Moon

When the moon is in Aries, you are motivated by fresh starts, forging new paths and bravely leading the way for others. You are encouraged to trust your gut and boldly go where no witch has gone before. However, while you feel independent, bold, and energetic, your impulse control isn't the best. You can get a little reckless with both actions and words.

NEW MOON IN ARIES: The Aries new moon is the first new moon of the astrological new year, when the sun is also in Aries, truly making it a period of new beginnings. This new moon not only allows you to plant the seeds for the next six months, but also sets the whole year—so really think about the life you wish to create for yourself and take small actions towards it.

FULL MOON IN ARIES: Known as the hunter moon, the Aries full moon usually occurs in early autumn, when the sun is in Libra. This is when you "harvest" the seeds you planted in March and see what you can use for the upcoming winter—or move on if your goals didn't quite work out. It is also the time to see where you used your energies and talents over the last six months and whether they panned out.

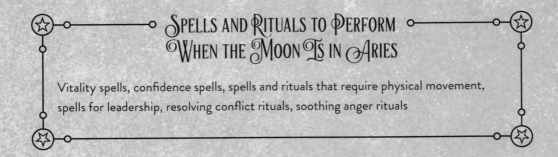

Spells and Rituals to Perform When the Moon Is in Aries

Vitality spells, confidence spells, spells and rituals that require physical movement, spells for leadership, resolving conflict rituals, soothing anger rituals

Taurus Moon

When the moon is in Taurus, it is your opportunity to slow down and take life at a steady pace. You can stop and enjoy life, from savoring a good cup of tea to feeling the grass under your feet. This is a comforting, restful time as you seek security and reconnect with your basic senses. However, make sure you don't get too comfortable and get stuck in bad habits.

NEW MOON IN TAURUS: Occurring mid-spring during Taurus season, the Taurus new moon helps you work toward your goals and aspirations in tangible ways. From vision boarding to spell casting, you are encouraged to put in the physical labor to achieve your heart's desire.

FULL MOON IN TAURUS: Known as the beaver moon, this full moon occurs in mid-autumn, during Scorpio season. The Taurus full moon encourages you to ground yourself and use all your senses to really savor your time here on Earth. Get back to the basics and enjoy what you have achieved—even if it's just staying alive.

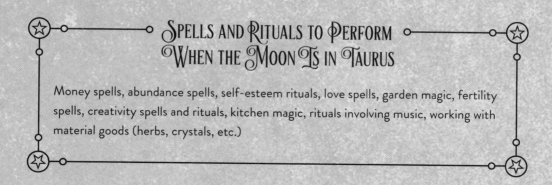

Spells and Rituals to Perform When the Moon Is in Taurus

Money spells, abundance spells, self-esteem rituals, love spells, garden magic, fertility spells, creativity spells and rituals, kitchen magic, rituals involving music, working with material goods (herbs, crystals, etc.)

Gemini Moon

When the moon is in Gemini, you can communicate with ease, especially when you're talking about your feelings and emotions. Whether you're writing, speaking, or just thinking, you are motivated to learn and share your knowledge with others. Your curiosity takes the wheel as you are encouraged to learn more and chat with your coven members. However, it can also make you overthink, feel restless, and become fickle.

NEW MOON IN GEMINI: Occurring at the end of spring, during Gemini season, the new moon in Gemini can function as a brainstorming session, giving you great ideas for the future. This is less of a "planning" phase and more of a "big picture ideas" period in time, so don't get too worked up over the details; allow yourself to think big.

FULL MOON IN GEMINI: Known as the cold moon, the Gemini full moon occurs at the end of autumn, when the sun is in Sagittarius. After spending six months "thinking," it's time to roll up your sleeves, actually pick something, and get to work. Focus on the minute details and put in the energy to make it a reality.

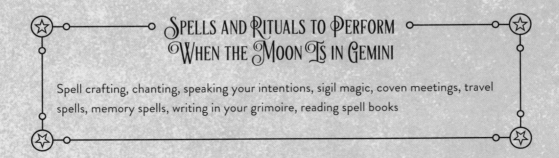

Spells and Rituals to Perform When the Moon Is in Gemini

Spell crafting, chanting, speaking your intentions, sigil magic, coven meetings, travel spells, memory spells, writing in your grimoire, reading spell books

Cancer Moon

As Cancer's ruling planet, the moon feels most at home in this sign. Because of this, we all have an urge to stay in our own homes during this time. It's a time to reach out to family members, nurture yourself, and just allow your body and spirit to rest and recharge where you feel safe. However, this moon phase can also make you extra emotional, moody, and a little more clingy than usual.

NEW MOON IN CANCER: Occurring during the early summer, when the sun is in Cancer, you keep your dreams and desires close to the vest and plant them in private. This isn't a time for big splashy announcements, but to quietly nurture your intentions at home.

FULL MOON IN CANCER: Known as the wolf moon, this is typically the first full moon of the new calendar year, when the sun is in Capricorn. What you held close during the new moon finally comes into fruition during the full moon. You can become public about what you manifested for yourself. Publicly claim it!

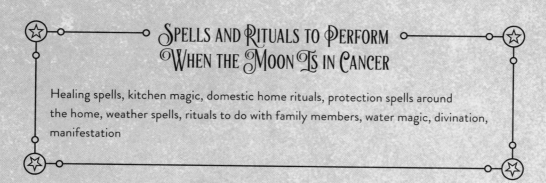

Spells and Rituals to Perform When the Moon Is in Cancer

Healing spells, kitchen magic, domestic home rituals, protection spells around the home, weather spells, rituals to do with family members, water magic, divination, manifestation

Leo Moon

The Leo moon encourages you to get in touch with your "inner child" and allow yourself to have fun. You can express yourself better during this time as you put your passion and abundance of energy into creative endeavors and find ways to shine. It's also a day of grand gestures and revealing your true feelings. However, it can also be a period of drama and seeking attention in unhealthy ways.

NEW MOON IN LEO: Occurring during the middle of summer, when the sun is in Leo, the new moon in Leo is a time of self-expression. It's a time where you begin something new—a relationship, an idea, or a goal—and put it into the spotlight to grow. Manifest and conjure with your heart open. Ask, "What makes me feel alive?"

FULL MOON IN LEO: Known as the snow moon, Leo's full moon typically occurs in mid-winter, when the sun is in Aquarius. When the full moon is in Leo, things really heat up as your heart is more open, and you're really in your feelings. It's no surprise that this moon usually occurs around Valentine's Day. The seeds of love and ambition are finally coming to bloom, and you can celebrate this love and success with the world.

Spells and Rituals to Perform When the Moon Is in Leo

Love spells, performing rituals, manifesting good vibes, rituals to reconnect with your inner child, spells for courage, candle magic, abundance spells, confidence spells, being generous, creative spell casting

Virgo Moon

When the moon is in Virgo, you often take the most practical approach to life, organizing your life and rethinking some of your hasty plans. In this phase, you work hard, noticing the smaller details, and are able to help others. However, this is also when your inner perfectionist comes out to play, making you overanalyze, worry, and be critical towards everyone—especially yourself.

NEW MOON IN VIRGO: The new moon in Virgo occurs during the end of the summer, when the sun is in Virgo; however, it's a little different from most new moons. Instead of planting seeds and setting intentions, you harvest ideas, goals, and even achievements. This is a time to look at what you cultivated and ask, "Where do I go from here?" It's a time to strategize where to put your energy and skill going forward.

FULL MOON IN VIRGO: Known as the worm moon, this full moon typically occurs at the end of winter, when the sun is in Pisces. This is a time to get lost in your thoughts and dream a little about what you truly desire. This daydreaming can help you understand those desires and start making a solid plan to make your fantasies a reality.

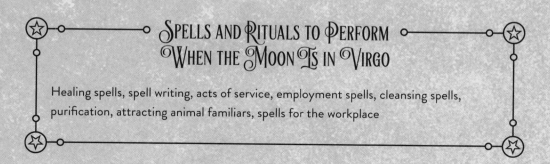

Spells and Rituals to Perform When the Moon Is in Virgo

Healing spells, spell writing, acts of service, employment spells, cleansing spells, purification, attracting animal familiars, spells for the workplace

Libra Moon

When the moon is in Libra, you are focused on creating balance and harmony through pleasant interactions with others, whether you solve problems diplomatically, create a comfortable home, or put emotions aside to reach a compromise. This is not the time for direct conflict or making big decisions as you are more indecisive and flightier. Instead, you are encouraged to create supportive relationships and work together.

NEW MOON IN LIBRA: The Libra new moon occurs during early autumn, when the sun is in Libra. This moon is all about establishing balance in your life. You are encouraged to use your common sense, put your feelings aside, and listen to all sides of a situation to create a peaceful solution. New relationships can be formed during this time, old relationships get a reset, and you can finally bury the hatchet.

FULL MOON IN LIBRA: Known as the pink moon, this is the first full moon of the astrological new year, occurring during the early spring when the sun is in Aries. The full moon in Libra helps you connect with your emotions and the people in your life. You can have total clarity in your relationships and see what is out of balance. It also allows you to love people with more depth.

Spells and Rituals to Perform When the Moon Is in Libra

Love spells, beauty spells, glamour magic, signing contracts, coven meetings, legal spells, spells for justice, handfasting ceremonies

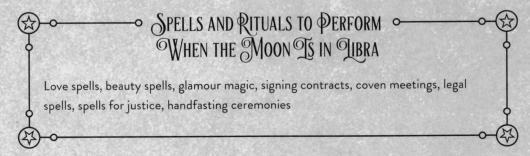

Scorpio Moon

When the moon is in Scorpio, all your intense emotions come out: passion, anger, sorrow, and pleasure are all felt on a personal level. Your intuition is increased as you can easily read between the lines to find the underlying cause of things (which makes you feel a little more powerful). While it can be a time of overcoming fears and bad habits, it can also be a time of manipulation, brooding, and plotting revenge.

NEW MOON IN SCORPIO: The Scorpio new moon occurs in mid-autumn, when the sun is also in Scorpio. This is the time to dive headfirst into the sea of emotions and see what lies beneath. It is also a time of big truths—even if it is something that you may not want to face. However, it is best to leave all your cards on the table and get everything off your chest so you are finally free to move forward.

FULL MOON IN SCORPIO: Known as the flower moon, the full moon in Scorpio occurs in mid-spring, when the sun is in Taurus. This is a very emotionally intense full moon. Whatever has been hidden in the shadows now becomes known, shaking up your relationships and your finances. However, these revelations are for the best as it gives you an opportunity to break bad habits and get rid of toxic people from your life.

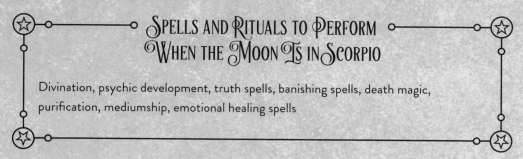

Spells and Rituals to Perform When the Moon Is in Scorpio

Divination, psychic development, truth spells, banishing spells, death magic, purification, mediumship, emotional healing spells

Sagittarius Moon

When the moon is in Sagittarius, you get an extra pick-me-up of optimism and positivity. This is a time for adventures, studying, and seeking out new visions of the life you want. It is time to look at the big picture without getting hung up on every little detail. Spontaneity is key, but try not to become too careless and overdo a good thing.

NEW MOON IN SAGITTARIUS: The new moon occurs during the end of autumn, when the sun is in Sagittarius, and is the most optimistic place for the new moon to be in. While the moon is at its darkest phase, Sagittarius encourages you to make your own light, to leave your painful past behind, and to step into your better and brighter future.

FULL MOON IN SAGITTARIUS: Often known as the strawberry moon, the Sagittarius full moon occurs in late spring, when the sun is in Gemini. Now is the time to focus on your long-term goals and hold yourself to a higher moral standard. You have spent the last six months letting go of the past; now you are learning the wonders your future can hold for you.

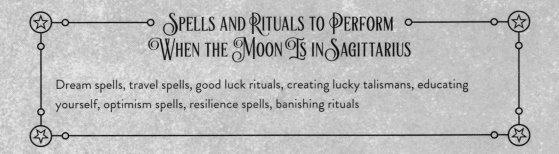

Spells and Rituals to Perform When the Moon Is in Sagittarius

Dream spells, travel spells, good luck rituals, creating lucky talismans, educating yourself, optimism spells, resilience spells, banishing rituals

Capricorn Moon

When the moon is in Capricorn, you become a little more serious and reserved than usual. This is a time for structure and making plans as your ambitions and desire for success increase. You are driven by the need to achieve something great during this phase. However, you can often become overwhelmed or pessimistic, and you can quickly burn out in your quest for success.

NEW MOON IN CAPRICORN: Usually the first new moon of the calendar year, the new moon in Capricorn occurs when the sun is in Capricorn, making it an extra critical time to set intentions and start making substantial changes to your life. This is an ideal time to set big goals as your increased drive and ambition will help you work towards them to get to the top. The new moon also gives you an increase in patience and discipline, so use it well.

FULL MOON IN CAPRICORN: Often known as the buck moon, the full moon in Capricorn occurs during the early summer, when the sun is in Cancer. During this full moon, you must work harder to finish what you started six months ago. This is not the time to settle for "no," but to tackle obstacles once and for all.

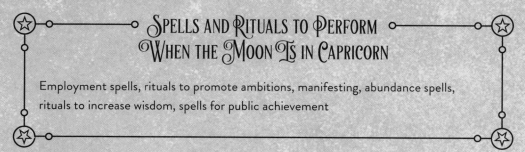

Spells and Rituals to Perform When the Moon Is in Capricorn

Employment spells, rituals to promote ambitions, manifesting, abundance spells, rituals to increase wisdom, spells for public achievement

Aquarius Moon

When the moon is in Aquarius, you are receptive to new and unusual things. Your eyes are open to what needs to be improved, even giving you unique ideas on how to solve the problems troubling you. You look to the future, brainstorming, making progressive changes, and being original. However, it can be hard to stick to a schedule, and you may turn people off with your "out there" ideas.

NEW MOON IN AQUARIUS: Occurring in mid-winter, when the sun is in Aquarius, the new moon in Aquarius encourages you to break free from what's holding you back. You can expand your vision and see multiple versions of the future that can be possible for you. However, you need to keep your feet on the ground, so you don't get overwhelmed with your ideas.

FULL MOON IN AQUARIUS: Often known as the sturgeon moon, the full moon in Aquarius occurs during mid-summer, when the sun is in Leo. The full moon in Aquarius reminds you that you are a part of a bigger collective: your coven, your power, your fellow human beings, and even Mother Earth in general. Your actions affect and benefit everyone the right way, so use that energy to better your community.

Spells and Rituals to Perform When the Moon Is in Aquarius

Friendship spells, technology spells, breaking bad habits, spells for problem-solving, meeting new people spells, group spells, coven meetings, luck spells

Pisces Moon

When the moon is in Pisces, you become more compassionate and sensitive, and your intuition increases as you imagine a world of unlimited possibilities. During this phase, your spiritual awareness is increased, and you feel a little more connected to the universe. However, it can also be difficult to tell between fantasy and reality, so use your gut when making decisions as it can be easy to trick yourself.

NEW MOON IN PIECES: Usually occurring during late spring, when the sun is in Pisces, the new moon in Pisces inspires you to imagine the future you want to bring to life. This is typically the last new moon of the astrological calendar, giving you a moment to fantasize about the new year and what you want to achieve. It is also an ideal time for healing old emotional wounds so you can become your best self. This is the new moon to spend alone and reflect.

FULL MOON IN PISCES: Known as the harvest moon, the full moon in Pisces typically occurs at the end of summer, when the sun is in Virgo. The full moon in Pisces is a time for compassion and lending a hand to those who need it. It is also a time to use your inspiration and take tangible steps to make your dreams a reality.

Spells and Rituals to Perform When the Moon Is in Pisces

Divination, strengthening psychic abilities, reversing bad luck, finding lost items, past lives rituals and reading, cord cutting spells, water magic, healing spells

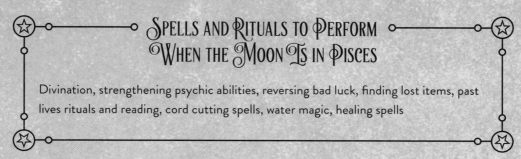

New Moon Ritual

The new moon is one of the best times to perform a ritual, especially if you are trying to set an intention or start a new chapter in your life. You can perform this ritual during any and all new moons, but it has a greater potency if you perform it when the moon is in the same sign as your natal moon. So, if you are a Taurus moon, you would do this ritual during the Taurus new moon.

MATERIALS

- Enough space to sit comfortably (preferably on the floor)
- Sandalwood incense mist
- Crystals associated with the zodiac sign the moon is in
- Paper
- Pen
- White candle
- Lighter

Optional:

- Candle snuffer

1 Light the sandalwood incense or spray the room with the mist to cleanse the room and help ground yourself.

2 Take the crystals, pen, and paper, and sit on the floor. Place the crystals around you in a circle. If you wish, hold one in your left hand, especially if you are looking to manifest the properties of that stone.

3 Take a few more grounding breaths. When you're ready, write out everything you wish to manifest during this lunar cycle, as though you already have them. For example, if you are looking to manifest a job, write, "I'm so happy that I'm working at a job I love where I am treated with respect." If you do not have a pen and paper, just think about what you desire.

4 When you're finished, take a few more calming breaths, then say, out loud, the following: "Dearest Luna, I come to thee, asking humbly that we can both start anew. That my dream can become my reality with a little help and wisdom from you. Here is who I am becoming during this next phase." Then read everything off your list or speak out everything you hope to manifest.

5 Stand up and light the candle. As you light it, say, "With this light, I'm creating the spark of my new beginnings. I'm leaving the darkness and stepping into the light of my future. So mote it be."

6 Watch the candle burn for a few minutes, thinking of everything you are trying to achieve during the next six months. When you feel ready, put the candle out. Close the circle and place the crystals and your list on your altar to charge.

FULL MOON RITUAL

When the moon is at its full visibility, it is also at its most potent, and we can feel the full force of its power here on earth. It's important to hold a ritual to celebrate the moon's power and use some of its magic in your spell work. You can do this ritual during any full moon. For best results, perform it when the full moon is in the same sign as your natal moon. So, if your moon is in Leo, you would do this during the Leo full moon.

MATERIALS

- A place where you can see the moon, either outside facing the moon or near a window
- Crystals associated with the sign the full moon is in
- Clean, clear water in a mason jar (or any jar)

Optional:
- Music

1 Go where you can see the moon, preferably outside, where you can bask in her light; just facing a window when the moon is out is fine too, just so you have enough space.

2 Cleanse your space and cast a circle. Place the crystals and the water in the moonlight so they can be charged.

3 Take a few deep breaths to steady yourself. As you ground yourself, think of all the things that this lunar cycle has given you. How has your life been different from six months ago? What are you happy about? What are you sad about? Allow those changes to flow through you.

4 When you are ready, let your body start to move: this can be dancing, it could be walking around, it can even be stretching your body towards the moon. Do whatever feels natural to you. If you have music, play it now.

5 Now that you've got your body warmed up, say, "Dearest Luna, I am here to honor your power and to bask in your light. Thank you for all the blessings I have received and the power I have used to achieve my desires." Then list everything for which you are grateful. The positive outcomes. The hard lessons you have learned. Everything that has gotten you to this point.

6 When you're finished, take the water and gesture it towards the moon, saying, "Thank you, Mother Moon, for all the blessings I have received. With this sip, I'll increase my personal power and become able to achieve all that I need. Everything I need is already within me." Take a sip.

7 When you're done, do a little more dancing if you feel like it. When you're ready, end the ritual with a small bow or curtsy towards the moon and say, "So mote it be."

8 Close the circle and cleanse your space. Leave the crystals and water on your windowsill to charge by the light of the full moon. Use the moon water for any upcoming spells.

4

THE PLANETS:
THE GUIDING FORCES OF YOUR LIFE

While Wiccans worship the moon, there are several other planets and celestial bodies that rule over our lives. Astrologers have been following the planets through the astrology signs for ages to understand their effects on our world: how we communicate, what is currently driving us, and even when we fall in love. When we know where the planets are, we can use them for our magical benefits, from the best time to cast an abundance spell to when we should avoid hexing people and instead work on our craft. We can also try bringing the energies of certain planets into our spell work and rituals by using the crystals and herbs associated with each planet.

In the following chapters, we will look at the influence of the sun, Mercury, Venus, Mars, Jupiter, and Saturn on our lives and our magic, and how they move through each sign. While Uranus, Neptune, and Pluto are important planets and have their own influences on our lives, they are more associated with the modern system of astrology, and Wicca focuses on the traditional systems of astrology. Uranus, Neptune, and Pluto also move slowly, taking years to get through a single sign, so tracking them isn't as difficult or necessary as tracking a fast-moving planet like Mercury.

In the time before technology, tracking the movements of planets was difficult because you needed to do a lot of math and have access to a decent telescope. However, thanks to modern technology, tracking the planets is just an online search away. If you're curious about what planets are currently in what sign, refer to the resource section (page 168) for websites that track the planets movements.

Retrogrades

If you've even just a little familiar with astrology, you've probably heard of retrogrades (usually in a negative spirit). While retrogrades have a scary reputation, they are not as bad as people make them out to be. A retrograde is simply when a planet appears to be traveling backward in the sky. However, the planet isn't really moving backward; that's just how it looks from our view on earth. Despite this, a planet's retrograde has actual effects on us. A retrograde can reshuffle a different area of our lives, turning things upside down with delays and changes. It can affect our magic too. For example, you wouldn't want to perform a money spell when Venus is in retrograde because it won't be as effective, or your spells may take extra time to manifest with Mars in retrograde. So pay close attention to any retrograde before you do any important casting. (We will look at retrogrades more in each planet's section.)

Still, retrogrades are not all bad. They can help open your eyes to the changes you need to make and encourage you to slow down and take stock in the important things in your life, as they can change in an instant.

The Sun

Okay, so the sun is not a planet at all. It is a star. However, because the Earth revolves around the sun and the sun is the thing that keeps us all alive, it is easy to say that the sun is fairly important. As witches honor and celebrate the moon, witches also need to honor and recognize the sun for the abundant light, warmth, and energy it brings to us. While the moon moves in cycles, the sun's power is whole, shining brightly.

CRYSTALS ASSOCIATED WITH THE SUN: Carnelian, orange calcite, sunstone, tiger's eye

HERBS ASSOCIATED WITH THE SUN: Angelica, juniper, rosemary, sunflowers

In astrology, the sun represents the spirit of life. It is associated with the self, energy, creativity, and vitality. When the sun moves through a particular sign, you will feel the energy of that sign, even if it isn't your sun sign. The sun is all about energy and what we do with it, and vibration matters. For example, when the sun is in Aries, it's important to take advantage of those feelings of boldness and courage the sun gives off so you can start new projects and take calculated risks. If you don't, it will take a whole year to feel that exact energy again.

The Sun Through the Signs

The sun moves through a single sign every thirty days through a whole calendar year and does not go through any retrogrades.

The Sun in Aries

 When the sun energizes fiery Aries, your magic is enthusiastic and spontaneous, motivated to conquer all that's in your way. You are interested in initiating new things in life, from spells to goals. Your magic is bold, pioneering, and innocent as you are open to the wonders and possibilities around you. You feel powerful and invincible, which can make you reckless and impulsive. Fortunately, you can always bounce back.

The Sun in Taurus

 When the sun is in Taurus, your magic moves at a slow and steady pace. You are more methodical when it comes to your practice and savor every step of the way. You are encouraged to take your time, to use all your senses in your craft. Determination and stamina are key to your success, but it can lead to stubbornness and possession.

The Sun in Gemini

 When the sun is in Gemini, you are driven by an insatiable drive for knowledge as you are curious about everything and anything. Your energies are scattered as you are interested in various subjects, from tea readings to enchantments. While it is not ideal for casting major spells, it's a perfect time to explore all of your options and adapt to whatever life throws at you.

The Sun in Cancer

 When the sun is in Cancer, you become a little more protective of your magic, with your intuition on high alert. You tend to take care of your home and your family, and do things that make you feel safe. You nurture your craft and tend to your magic to make it grow stronger. However, your emotions are strong; one bad mood can spell chaos for everyone.

The Sun in Leo

 The sun is back home when it is in Leo, and you can bask in the warmth of a happy reunion. This is an ideal time to celebrate your magic and find your own way to shine. You perform rituals like you are acting on stage, boldly decorating yourself and your altar with colors and trinkets. It is the time to be your most authentic self.

The Sun in Libra

 When the sun is in Libra, "me" quickly becomes "we" in every aspect of life. Your magic helps to form compromises and partnerships that are balanced and fair to all involved. Life is beautiful right now and you can use magic to create your own beauty. However, this is not the best time to make decisions as you'll be too consumed with the choices.

The Sun in Virgo

 Your energy shifts to the finer details of your life as you hone your magic with care when the sun is in Virgo. You can now clearly analyze your life and see what needs fixing and how you can improve things. Your magic is practical as you learn to perfect your skills and organize your surroundings without stressing yourself out.

The Sun in Scorpio

 The sun in Scorpio creates an intense period as you use your magic to transform your life in almost every way. Your intuition is strong, perfect for divination, mediumship, or trying to figure yourself out. This can be a powerful healing time or a time to seek revenge and settle scores—the choice is yours.

The Sun in Sagittarius

When the sun is in Sagittarius, you long to understand the vibrations of the world. You are a seeker of knowledge, using your magic to unlock the truths about the world. Everything you do right now is done with optimism and universal love. Your magic thrives off hope and faith. However, with all this extra energy, passion, and courage, it is easy to burn out and hurt yourself.

The Sun in Aquarius

When the sun is in Aquarius, your magic is drawn to all things original and innovative. You stray from tradition to forge your own path. You are attracted to the collective energy of communities, and the universe as a whole, as you consider how you can make a difference. You crave freedom, but your lofty goals may be a little out of reach.

The Sun in Capricorn

When the sun is in Capricorn, your magic is focused and determined as you wield your power to achieve your ambitions. You are focused on taking on a lot of new responsibilities during this time, but it's nothing that you cannot handle. You can endure so much as you work towards your long-held goals. Every single action is important.

The Sun in Pisces

When the sun is in Pisces, your magic and energy are influenced by altruism and emotions. You can feel the emotions of others as easily as you can feel your own, which influences your magic in both positive and negative ways. You rely on your wisdom to make choices and give your energy to others with devotion, even if it does drain you dry.

A Ritual to Harness The Energy of the Sun

Like the moon, the sun is a powerful cleansing and healing energy that you can use to charge your crystals, tools, and yourself. An added bonus is that you don't have to wait for a full moon to get the complete benefits of its powers. All you need is a summer day. Use this ritual to help bring sunny and positive vibrations to your magic and give your mood a major lift. For best results, perform this spell on a Sunday, as it is the day that the sun rules.

MATERIALS

- A sunny day when it's nice enough to be outside
- Carnelian, orange calcite, sunstone, and tiger's eye (or crystals that correspond with the sign the sun is currently in)
- Sunflower petals
- Rosemary sprig
- Mason jar full of clean, clear water

1 Go outside and find a nice spot in the sun, preferably by a tree facing east, but it's okay to use whatever you have to work with.

2 Place the crystals in the four corners, like on a compass (north, east, south, west). Stand in the center and take some deep grounding breaths.

3 When you're ready, toss the sunflower petals in the air in front of you, letting them scatter on the ground. As they fall, say, "Dear sun, I humbly ask of you to brighten up my magic with your eternal life. Let your golden rays shine on me."

4 Now take the sprig of rosemary and, keeping it close to your heart, say, "With these offerings of sunflowers and rosemary, I hope you will let a little joy, light, and energy flow through me like the water in my cup. Let me be strong. Let me absorb light. Let me be what I need to be. So mote it be."

5 Put the sprig of rosemary on the ground and sit down. Hold the mason jar of water in your hands, making sure that it is directly in the sunlight. Close your eyes and think of your magic flowing through your body. Imagine it getting brighter and brighter, glowing with the sun's energy. Imagine the spells you'll cast, the rituals you'll be performing with that energy. Let it wash over you.

6 When you're ready, close the circle. Keep that water as sun water and use it for teas, spells, and ritual baths to soak in the sun's energy when needed.

Mercury

Known as the planet of communication, Mercury doesn't just influence the way we talk but also how we think, process information, and create. When Mercury moves through the zodiac, it reflects the sign it stays in, sending its vibrations to us here on Earth. It can help explain why sometimes we have a challenging time processing information, or why it feels like something major is happening every day on the news.

In witchcraft, Mercury helps with your spell crafting, encouraging you to choose what spells to use, how to say them, or even what you should be avoiding right now. Mercury is your voice, not only how you personally communicate, but how you communicate to the universe as a whole.

CRYSTALS ASSOCIATED WITH MERCURY:
Blue lace agate, jasper, moldavite, peridot

HERBS ASSOCIATED WITH MERCURY: Dill, lavender, licorice, marjoram

Mercury Through The Signs

Mercury is one of the fastest-moving planets, moving through a sign every two weeks. However, it is slowed down a little by its three yearly retrogrades.

Mercury in Aries

 Your words and thinking are rapid and passionate when Aries is in Mercury. It is easy to cast spells and even create whole new rituals, simply because you feel like it. Your ideas are pioneering and innovative, even though you can shoot your mouth off if you aren't careful. Don't cast hexes and curses so quickly; they'll backfire on you.

Mercury in Taurus

 Your thinking and communication are solid, stable, and down-to-earth, as you take your time before you cast any major spells. This is a time to cast deliberately, thinking things through so you don't waste your precious energy on things that will not serve you in the long term. You prefer the tried-and-true magical methods and can be very reluctant to make necessary changes.

Mercury in Gemini

 Mercury is at home in Gemini, so your words flow easily through you during this time—especially all verbal communication. You are hungry for knowledge during this time and can process information quicker. This is an ideal time to learn new methods of magic quickly, cast short spells, and socialize with other witches to gain information. However, you won't get too deep with anyone or anything.

Mercury in Cancer

 All communication and thoughts take on an emotional edge when Mercury is in Cancer; everything takes on a deeper meaning. Your magic can manifest things that hold deep meaning to your heart. It is difficult to be objective now as emotions run high. However, this is ideal for home and protection spells or for sharing rituals with family members.

Mercury in Leo

 'Tis the season for confidence spells as you'll feel bold and brave. You are expressive, making it ideal for grand rituals, mantras, and manifestation. Sure, you can create some serious drama during this time, but it will be very entertaining. Remember to not go so overboard with your spells and magic that it becomes too big for you to manage. Listen to the advice your elders give you.

Mercury in Libra

 It is all about negotiating and diplomacy when Mercury is in Libra. Your spells and thoughts are focused on how you can find peace, balance, and harmony in your life. You can look at all points of view and use your magic to make a compromise (or find your perfect match). However, this isn't a good time for making decisions as you'll have difficulty making up your mind.

Mercury in Virgo

 Mercury is also home when it enters Virgo, though it is easier to express yourself through writing than in spoken words. This is an ideal time to write out your spells and intentions and start or add to a grimoire. Spells and rituals are done with precision as you cross everything off your magical "to-do" list. While the devil is in the details, don't ruin your positive energy trying to make everything "perfect."

Mercury in Scorpio

 Your communication and thoughts are probing and intense when Mercury is in exacting Scorpio. You are on a quest to find all the skeletons in all the closets, including your own. This is an ideal time to practice divination and mediumship as you try to get your answers from otherworldly sources. However, you can become obsessive or vindictive, and seek revenge.

Mercury in Sagittarius

 When Mercury is in Sagittarius, you are interested in a wide range of topics as you have a deep desire to understand things, from why we do candle spells to why we worship the moon. You develop a life philosophy, evaluate your views on the world, and find comfort in your faith. However, you might not be as precise as you desire as you are so focused on the "big picture" that you miss the little things.

Mercury in Capricorn

 When Mercury is in Capricorn, your thinking is methodical, and your communication is serious and practical. You know exactly what you want and are willing to do the work to get it. Important decisions are made as you use magic to play the long game. You need to be logical and realistic about what you try to manifest, so you don't end up disappointed.

Mercury in Aquarius

 You are your most original and inventive self when Mercury is in Aquarius. You are sick of the "traditional" way of doing things and are inspired to make your own rules and rituals. It's an ideal time for techno spells and reshaping your coven as your thoughts are more progressive. However, remember to think about the community when you update your magical practices.

Mercury in Pisces

 Your imagination and intuition come to the surface when Mercury is in Pisces. You are hyper-attuned to the world around you, feeling every emotion deeply. This is a time for writing imaginative spells, visualizing what you want, and just living in your daydreams for a little bit. Go with your gut as you focus on more spiritual matters than practical ones.

MERCURY IN RETROGRADE

Mercury goes into retrograde three to four times a year and lasts for around three weeks. It is the most common retrograde that actively affects our daily lives. When Mercury is in retrograde, our communication, technology, travel, and logic get disrupted as we must deal with delays, miscommunication, misinformation, and misunderstandings. Projects stall, breakups occur, and our schedules are thrown off.

Needless to say, it's not an ideal time for any form of spell casting. You should perform protection spells before the retrograde and focus on being adaptable and open to changes during the retrograde. Here is what the retrograde means for different signs.

MERCURY'S RETROGRADE IN AIR SIGNS

Gemini, Libra, Aquarius: This retrograde is going to affect your logic more than anything. Your thinking won't be as clear as you like it to be, and you tend to suffer from misinformation and lack key knowledge. It's easy to believe rumors and take fiction as fact. Don't make any major decisions right now and back up all of your files (especially if you have a digital grimoire).

MERCURY'S RETROGRADE IN FIRE SIGNS

Aries, Leo, Sagittarius: This retrograde can quite literally "blow up" in your face if you are not careful. Tempers easily flare and you can say cutting things you don't mean. Passions burn high and bridges can easily become ashes. It can be hard to keep a hold of your temper with everything going wrong but don't pick fights without all the information first.

MERCURY'S RETROGRADE IN EARTH SIGNS

Taurus, Virgo, Capricorn: This retrograde can shake up your carefully planted roots and mess with your stability and comfort. This is not an ideal time for traveling as you'll need to be "grounded" in one place. This retrograde can also affect your work ethic, finances, and comfort. However, it does encourage you to get back to basics.

MERCURY'S RETROGRADE IN WATER SIGNS

Cancer, Scorpio, Pisces: Your feelings are extra sensitive when Mercury goes into retrograde in water signs. Everything is felt more, and you can easily be injured by the smallest slight—real or perceived. Emotions are harder to read, and everything feels more confusing. Stay home as much as you can.

We could all use the gift of gab at one point or another. Voicing your desires can help them manifest, and talking out a difficult problem can help you produce a solution. Try this spell if you have an issue that you could really use Mercury's help on (having a difficult conversation, solving a problem, trying to study, etc.). For best results, perform it on a Wednesday, as it is ruled by Mercury.

MATERIALS

- Lavender tea or lavender-flavored coffee
- Mug (preferably yellow)
- Teaspoon
- Sewing needle
- Yellow candle
- Lighter
- Crystal associated with Mercury (or associated with the sign that Mercury's currently in)

Optional:
- Pen and paper
- Candle snuffer

1 Make your coffee or tea the way you normally prepare it. Stir it three times clockwise, saying, "With this brew, I open up the lines of communication, letting the words flow through."

2 Sit at your altar or at a table. With the needle, carve the symbol for Mercury into the candle.

3 Light the candle and say, "Dear Mercury, I invite you today to spill the tea and chat away. Let me tell you about my problems so you can give me a way to solve them. So mote it be."

4 Start talking! Speak about what you are trying to manifest, the spells you are trying to cast, or the issues you have been having. If this makes you feel a little silly, write it all down on paper. Just get it all out there while holding the crystal as you do.

5 When your drink is finished, say "thank you" and put out the candle. Do this regularly until you get the results you desire.

VENUS

While you're probably familiar with Venus as the Roman goddess of love and beauty, Venus is more than just the planet of love. Venus also rules over our finances, material possessions, what we are attracted to, what brings us pleasure, what we value, and our relationships. When Venus moves through a sign, we tend to take on the aesthetic of that sign, including the colors and materials that are associated with it. We also take on how that sign acts in relationships and how that sign spends money. Venus in Aries can make passionate hot love affairs, while Venus in Aquarius can make things a little cold. While Venus in Virgo encourages us to be thrifty, Venus in Sagittarius suggests spending all money on plane tickets. We are simply following the vibes.

Witches often call upon the energy of Venus when conjuring a love spell, so knowing where Venus is can help you choose if you are going to be having a fiery love affair or a slow-burn romance that could lead to a lifelong partnership. Venus is also great for money and abundance spells and just finding inspiration when decorating your altar or performing glamour magic.

> **CRYSTALS ASSOCIATED WITH VENUS:** Emerald, green aventurine, rhodonite, rose quartz
>
> **HERBS ASSOCIATED WITH VENUS:** Bergamot, hibiscus, mugwort, rose

Venus Through The Signs

Venus moves through a sign every four weeks and goes into retrograde once every eighteen months, and lasts for around six weeks.

Venus in Aries

 When Venus is in Aries, you're feeling extra amorous, falling in love with people you just met. This has a "love at first sight" vibe as you go after our crushes with desire and boldness. This is an ideal time to cast (ethical) love spells and manifest desires. However, love affairs and desire can burn out as quickly as they begin, so don't invest too much into them.

Venus in Taurus

 Venus is at home in Taurus; therefore, you feel safe and secure as you look for things and people that are steady. You have a strong appetite for pleasure, indulging in the finer things in life. This is an ideal time for casting abundance spells and rituals that require the use of all your senses. Love is expressed in physical ways but be mindful of getting jealous.

Venus in Gemini

 When Venus is in Gemini, you don't "fall in love" as much as you flirt and indulge in witty banter. Everyone is a potential love interest right now, but don't plan a whole future around them. This is a time for road trips, sending spells through texts, and having fun. However, hearts can be fickle, so don't cast any major spells or make big purchases.

Venus in Cancer

 Your heart is tender and soft when Venus is in Cancer, though it is protected by a hard surface to prevent a broken heart. You are more devoted than ever to your loved ones and to your craft, especially when magic can be used as a form of self-care and self-love. However, don't get too nostalgic thinking about lovers past, and block your ex now (thank me later).

VENUS IN LEO

 Your heart (and wallet) are wide open when Venus is in Leo as you are more generous with your time, love, money, and magic. This is a time of sizzling hot love affairs and extravagant purchases of outfits and crystals. However, it can be difficult to ask for or manifest money as you'll be too proud to take it. Still, it is an ideal time to speak what's in your heart.

VENUS IN LIBRA

 In one of its ruling signs, Venus is happy to be in Libra and can happily share that love with others. This is the time of entering relationships, casting glamour and ethical love spells, and making your space beautiful. However, despite this romantic vibe, it's not a super passionate time as you seek what "looks" good rather than what "feels" good.

VENUS IN VIRGO

 When Venus is in Virgo, love isn't something you feel but something you do. You are more willing to drop everything to help anyone in need without asking for everything you need. You spend your money on practical necessities and cast spells to improve your life, especially your health. However, you can be overly picky and critical of everything right now, which can drive lovers away.

VENUS IN SCORPIO

 Venus in Scorpio is a high-stakes period where the energy is "all or nothing." You feel everything with more intensity. Relationships develop and can get very serious very quickly as you bond over this passionate energy. While it is not the time for a binding spell, this is a great financial period, especially with manifesting money. However, try not to go to extremes with anything; you will regret them later.

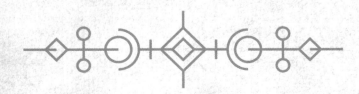

Venus in Sagittarius

 Your heart is open and honest when Venus is in Sagittarius. No longer tied down to one person or place, you are free to roam wherever the universe takes you. This is an excellent time for travel as you'll be spending most of your money on fulfilling your wanderlust. Speak your heart's truth in all your spell work.

Venus in Capricorn

 This is an ideal financial period as you work towards earning and saving for the dream life you have always wanted. It's an ideal time for abundance spells or placing protection spells on your wallet. On the romantic side, you are more interested in becoming a power couple than anything else. It's a good time to cast spells to keep lovers faithful and your love successful–whatever that means to you.

Venus in Aquarius

 It's the season of friends to lovers when Venus is in Aquarius, where the line between friendship and relationships is about to be blurred. You are more interested in experimenting with different types of relationships–only committing to things on your terms. This is an ideal time for networking, forming covens, and finding your own magical community that will make you feel accepted.

Venus in Pisces

 Love is forgiving and kind when Venus is in Pisces. You find compassion and affection for everyone in your life, making it such a tender and vulnerable period. You feel a deep longing for something you cannot define and may use dream magic and divination to help find the answers. However, it may be easy to get lost in delusions, so no love spells.

VENUS IN RETROGRADE

While Mercury has a big reputation for being a scary retrograde, Venus has the more powerful retrograde. That's because it affects our hearts and our wallets, which can be harder to heal from than a few misplaced words.

When Venus is in retrograde, you are forced to reevaluate all the commitments you've made. Which investments (financial, emotional, and magical) are paying off, and which aren't? While this is a very rough period, it does clear away any baggage you've been ignoring and force you to address underlying issues to move forward. However, this is not a great time for love, money, or glamour spells. Here's what Venus's retrograde means for different signs.

VENUS'S RETROGRADE IN AIR SIGNS

Gemini, Libra, Aquarius: When Venus is retrograde in an air sign, it's harder to tap into your emotions as you become detached. You may ignore red flags in relationships or have bills piling up. You'll need to have some tough conversations, but it can be difficult if you aren't acting with logic.

VENUS'S RETROGRADE IN EARTH SIGNS

Taurus, Virgo, Capricorn: Finances will be hit the hardest as your source of income gets disrupted. Relationships you thought were solid begin to crack and you'll have to work harder than ever to find a solution and make it work—or move on.

VENUS'S RETROGRADE IN FIRE SIGNS

Aries, Leo, Sagittarius: This is a very intense period as you swing from overly hot passion to sudden coolness. Relationships can easily blow up and you can burn through your savings with ease. It can be hard to pump the breaks when all you want to do is move forward—even if it hurts you.

VENUS'S RETROGRADE IN WATER SIGNS

Cancer, Scorpio, Pisces: You are caught up in a whirlwind of emotions as everything is felt much more deeply in a water sign. Your moods rule your life as you can easily enter toxic relationships, break up long-lasting relationships, and spend money to self-soothe. This retrograde is like a hurricane; you'll just have to hang in there.

Ruling over love, beauty, and material possessions, Venus loves the finer things in life. To honor both the planet and the goddess, use this spell to charm an amulet to bring the powers of Venus with you whenever you wear it. For best results, perform it on a Friday, as it is ruled by Venus.

MATERIALS

- Pendant necklace (preferably rose quartz or a heart-shaped pendant, otherwise something you're drawn to)
- Perfume (or bergamot, hibiscus, or rose-scented mist)

1 Charge and cleanse the space where you'll be working and the necklace.

2 With the pendant in your hands, take a good look at it. What is your intention? Are you using Venus's power for self-love? For attracting a suitor? Or attracting wealth? Or do you merely just want to hold Venus close to you? There are no wrong answers here, but be honest with what you want.

3 When you're ready, take the perfume or spray and say, "Dear lovely Venus. I call to you to have your enchanting powers flow into my amulet. Give me a token of love so I can achieve my highest good." Repeat this three times.

4 When you're done, wear your necklace until Venus moves into the next sign.

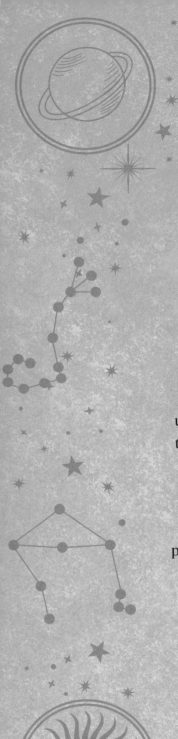

MARS

The red planet next door packs quite the punch in the astrological world, being named after the Roman god of war. However, Mars isn't just about picking fights and unleashing our anger (though that's a big part of it). Mars is where our passions lie and where our drives are. It also shows what motivates us, and it deals with desires, especially physical and sexual desires.

CRYSTALS ASSOCIATED WITH MARS: Bloodstone, hematite, ruby, sapphire
HERBS ASSOCIATED WITH MARS: Basil, black pepper, cumin, nettle

Witches can strongly benefit from harnessing the energy and power of Mars in any spell and ritual they do because its energy is raw and passionate. However, it is especially useful when working with feelings of anger and rage. You can feel your most powerful when you work with Mars, reminding yourself (and everyone else) that a witch bows to no one. The sign that Mars is in can help you decide how you should step into your personal power and in what ways.

Mars Through the Signs

It takes Mars about six weeks to move through a single zodiac sign and goes through a retrograde period once every twenty-six months, lasting for eighty days.

Mars in Aries

 Mars is right at home in Aries so your natural passion, energy, and drive get a major boost as you feel you can tackle anything and everything that comes your way. Your magic is stronger within you, crackling through your veins. You feel courageous, competitive, and ready to win anything, though you can take unnecessary risks that could hurt you. Be careful with what you manifest, especially in anger.

Mars in Taurus

 When Mars is in Taurus you are working at a slower pace, but it doesn't mean that you aren't achieving something. In fact, your resilience and determination are stronger than ever as you push back against the forces that are pushing you. You are operating on the defense during this period as you patiently work towards your goals... though you can be a little hardheaded about certain things.

Mars in Gemini

 Your energy is more versatile and adaptable when Mars is in Gemini as your energy can flow into multiple different projects and spells, from developing a new enlightenment spell to coming up with the perfect comeback. However, you aren't the most focused, and it can be hard to reach any type of goal with scattered energies. Grounding and meditating are needed to take advantage of this abundance of energy.

Mars in Cancer

 You are very protective of the people you love when Mars is in Cancer, willing to defend your home at all costs. Your energy and passion are deep as you deal with mood swings and strong emotions. Finding peace in nature (especially by the water) can help ground you as you care for your energy and passions. On the bright side, your visualizations can easily manifest.

Mars in Leo

 This is BIG MOOD as Mars in bold Leo is bright and intense. Everything that you do is loud and filled with passion and self-confidence. Your ego may increase as you feel like everything you do is of the highest importance. Your drive is strong but be careful with the spells that you cast; they can easily blow up in your face.

Mars in Virgo

 Mars is hard at work when it's in Virgo, and so are you. Your energy, drive, and passion are focused on what you can achieve, going over everything with a fine-tooth comb. Satisfaction comes from doing something well, from performing an intensive ritual to casting a spell. Mars in Virgo asks, "Do you want it done fast, or do you want it done right?"

Mars in Libra

 It's a period for legally binding contacts when Mars is in Libra. Whether you are performing binding spells or trying to resolve conflict, your inner lawyer witch comes out to bring peace and form partnerships. This is a time of spirited debates, but there's also a level of passive-aggressiveness that can cut like a knife. Keeping the peace can be difficult but rewarding in the long run.

Mars in Scorpio

 Mars is at home in Scorpio, giving us all an extra boost of energy, passion, and drive. However, unlike Mars in Aries, you don't loudly dive into things. Instead, you play the long game. You let your anger simmer until it's the perfect time to strike with deadly accuracy. This is a great time for spell work as you are driven by perseverance and single-minded drive.

Mars in Sagittarius

 This is a period for wide-open spaces when Mars is in Sagittarius as you need to explore nature to feel at peace. Freedom is your main priority as anything restricting will have you in a rage. There is a restlessness in your heart, and as you search for freedom, you may have to cut all the ties that bind and embrace your inner adventurer.

Mars in Aquarius

 Mars in Aquarius can be a bit of a hit-or-miss period as you have so many amazing and unique ideas that sometimes don't quite pan out with the erratic energy levels. You deal less with raw feelings and are more driven towards intellectual interests that truly light the spark of passion within. Don't be afraid to try something new with your rituals and craft.

Mars in Capricorn

 Energy and passions take a serious tone when Mars is in Capricorn. Use your magic deliberately, not wasting an ounce on petty feuds or short-lived pleasures. Consider every possible outcome before taking action, thinking about the future in everything you do. Your rage fuels you to victory one step at a time. However, the energy is a little cold and calculating.

Mars in Pisces

 When Mars is in Pisces you are driven towards spiritual quests as you try to understand the source that drives your intense emotions. You need to meditate, ground yourself, and even perform dream magic to tap into the core of your spiritual side. You are driven by your enthusiastic ideals that can easily be crushed by the cruel world, creating uneven energy levels and even hopelessness.

Mars in Retrograde

Mars goes into a retrograde once every twenty-six months and it is quite a doozy, especially since it lasts for around eighty days. Mars in retrograde is a difficult period because it's the planet of action. With Mars moving backward, it can create frustration, disappointment, and plenty of anger. It also dramatically shifts your motivation, making you directionless and even a little lazy when all your plans and projects get canceled. This isn't a great time for any spells that require a great amount of passion and drive. It's also a good idea to stay away from any activities involving sharp objects: haircuts, tattoos, cutting flowers, using an athame during rituals. Mars is the planet of war so stay away from anything that can be turned into a weapon.

MARS RETROGRADE IN AIR SIGNS

Gemini, Libra, Aquarius: Your intellectual energies will be scattered as it becomes hard to focus on anything. School and other forms of education will be difficult as you lose your drive and passion for learning. Relationships become cold and distant as you have a tough time connecting with people close to you.

MARS RETROGRADE IN EARTH SIGNS

Taurus, Virgo, Capricorn: Your core foundation is going to get rocked as things that you thought were steady and stable suddenly fall apart, almost without warning. Your work ethic is zapped as it is difficult to complete any goals because you are completely burnt out. Find comfort in nature.

MARS RETROGRADE IN FIRE SIGNS

Aries, Leo, Sagittarius: This is the worst element for Mars to retrograde in because our collective temper is at its worst. This is a period of deep anger without really any way to channel it in productive ways. You are angry for the sake of being angry and can easily burn your life down just to have something to do. Try to be kind to yourself so you may heal.

MARS RETROGRADE IN WATER SIGNS

Cancer, Scorpio, Pisces: Issues that you thought were over suddenly come back to the surface, raw and deeply tender. It is a time for tears and a time for getting even—though these attempts will not be successful as you will be too clouded by emotions. The only thing you can do is sit in your emotions and wait for them to pass.

The warrior planet can give you the energy, drive, and passion to help you achieve what you need and want to have done. If you need a little boost, try this spell to have the vibrations of Mars course through your veins. However, Mars wants you to give a little too. For best results, perform this spell on a Tuesday, as it is ruled by Mars.

MATERIALS

- A place big enough for you to move around in
- Red clothing that's comfortable to move in

Optional:
- Music (especially a workout playlist)

1 Cleanse and charge your space and put on the red clothing.

2 Stand in the center of your space with your feet firmly on the ground. Take a few deep breaths and visualize Mars in your mind and everything it represents. Then say, "Dear Mars, please grant the energy and raw power to tackle my obstacles like the warrior that I am."

3 Get moving! Whether you're doing yoga, strength training, cardio, kickboxing, or just dancing around, put on some music and just move and grove your body to the beat. As you move, think of that energy flowing through the universe, getting charged by Mars's power. Visualize yourself overcoming the challenges you're facing as you move.

4 Move around just enough that you're feeling energized but not overly tired or breathing heavily. Close your circle and use this energy and vibration to cast the spell you want using the magic of Mars.

JUPITER

As the largest planet in our solar system, Jupiter packs a powerful cosmic punch as it is the planet of abundance, luck, success, expansion, growth, and faith. If

CRYSTALS ASSOCIATED WITH JUPITER: Amethyst, lapis lazuli, lepidolite, yellow sapphire
HERBS ASSOCIATED WITH JUPITER: Cloves, dandelion, nutmeg, common sage

you're looking to perform a good luck spell, summon the energy of Jupiter. Looking for a little positivity after a dark period? Jupiter. Looking to perform a justice spell? Call upon Jupiter—it has your back through all things.

It takes Jupiter twelve years to go through the zodiac wheel, spending about one year in each sign. Jupiter is slowed down by its annual retrograde, where it spends about four months per year. While the zodiac sign that Jupiter is in is important, as it sets the tone of your year, it often doesn't directly affect your craft like some of the faster-moving planets do.

We could all use a little luck and prosperity in our lives. However, just like you have to make your own luck in this world, you also have to make your own oil that attracts luck to you. Here is an anointing oil that uses the energy of Jupiter to bring you the prosperity you need. For best results, make this prosperity oil on a Thursday, as it ruled by Jupiter.

MATERIALS

- Small bottle with a lid or cap (preferably amber glass)
- Olive oil
- Dried cloves, nutmeg, sage, dandelion root, or herbs that are associated with the sign that Jupiter is currently in

Optional:
- Peppermint essential oil

1 Fill the bottle ¾ full with olive oil.

2 Place the herbs and essential oil, if using, in the bottle and cap it.

3 Hold the bottle in your hands and say, "Dear Jupiter, grant me your wisdom and abundance of optimism to help me get a little lucky in life. Help me see my vision of success come to life. Let me prosper in all that I do. So mote it be."

4 Shake the bottle and leave it at your altar to charge. Use this prosperity oil to anoint money, candles, your altar, crystals, the papers you write spells on, or anything that needs an extra boost. However, make sure that you never let the bottle go empty. Continue to fill it with herbs and oil when needed.

SATURN

Don't let those mesmerizing rings fool you; Saturn is the tough taskmaster of the planets. In astrology, Saturn represents structures, discipline, and restrictions. It is the planet of boundaries, showing us what our limits are. Saturn is here to teach us a lesson—a lesson that we aren't always willing to learn. Because of that, Saturn has to be a little creative. It knows that experience is the best teacher, so it gives us difficult experiences as a teaching tool while showing us the obstacles we must face in this life and how to overcome them.

CRYSTALS ASSOCIATED WITH SATURN: Black obsidian, onyx, shungite, smoky quartz
HERBS ASSOCIATED WITH SATURN: Comfrey, garlic, St. John's wort, valerian

Saturn is also the planet of karmic returns, which is part of the reason witches enjoy using it in their karmic spells, rituals, and other justice-seeking spells. However, be very careful when using Saturn, as it represents both good and bad karma. Instead, witches should be using Saturn as a teacher, showing the boundary lines of your magic and working within them.

It takes Saturn twenty-eight to thirty years to move through the zodiac, staying in a single sign for around three years. It also goes into an annual retrograde for about four months. Because it is such a slow-moving planet, we don't focus our magic so much on which sign Saturn is in, but rather the vibrations we feel from the planet in general.

We have so many distractions that keep us from doing the things we need to be doing. We let people invade our personal space, we get torn away from our studies, and we let our magic scatter all around us. Fortunately, the rings of Saturn can give you the discipline and structure you need to set boundaries and finally focus. For best results, perform this spell on a Saturday, as it is ruled by Saturn.

1 Charge and cleanse your space. Place the rope on the floor in the shape of a circle.

2 Get in the circle and sit down. Take a few grounding breaths. Light the candle and hold the crystal, if you're using them.

3 When you are ready, say, "Dear Saturn, I call upon you to give me the strength to honor my boundaries. Help me form structures that help me stay focused and disciplined on what I need to do. I am safe here. So mote it be."

4 Start working on the task you brought. This is also a good time to have important conversations over the phone, text, or email, telling people what your personal boundaries are.

5 When you're done, close the circle and continue your day.

MATERIALS

- A quiet place
- Long piece of rope or string (long enough to form a circle you can sit in)
- Something you're supposed to be working on

Optional:
- Black candle (color associated with Saturn)
- Lighter
- Black obsidian (for protection and focus)

5

THE HOUSES

Have you ever read your horoscope and wondered, "How can they predict this? They must be making it up"? It is a common misconception that astrologers and astrology writers just make things up as they go along. That's actually quite far from the truth, as astrologers and astrology writers study the sky and use the patterns of the heavenly bodies to help predict events. Wiccans could benefit from learning this system so they can plan spells, know when to strengthen their magic, and help keep their future in their hands. But it's important to go beyond the zodiac signs, to learn about the astrological houses and their effects on your life and your magic.

As noted in the first part of this book, the zodiac is divided into twelve sections, each hosting a single zodiac sign. These segments are called houses and each house has an astrological sign that rules it, starting with Aries ruling the first house, Taurus ruling the second, and so on with Pisces ruling the twelfth house. Each of these houses has a unique set of traits and challenges that are associated with the sign.

Each house is also associated with a different aspect of life. The first six houses are the "personal houses" as they deal with our internal issues: body and appearance, handling finances, personal communication, family roots, self-expression, and routines. The last six houses are the "impersonal houses" as they deal with issues outside of ourselves: partnerships, changes, travel, career ambitions, social connections, and the subconscious mind. All of them together make up an entire life's journey.

As you may have noticed when looking at your birth chart, the chart is also on a wheel. This is known as a horoscope, where your birth chart is divided into twelve sections, sort of like the face of a clock. Start with your rising sign, which goes in your first house at 9:00, and move counterclockwise, following the order of the signs, from Aries to Pisces. For example, if you are a Virgo rising, your first house would be ruled by Virgo, then your second house would be ruled by Libra, etc. Each of these houses takes on the traits of the sign that rules it and highlights the areas of your life that you will focus on, where your gifts lie, and the obstacles you will need to overcome, especially if you have a bunch of natal planets in a particular house.

Horoscopes, the kind you read online or in magazines, are written using the rising sign to see what planets are currently transitioning through a sign and how that affects your life. For example, let's say that Mercury, the planet of communication, just entered Leo. If you are an Aquarius rising, Leo would be in your seventh house, or the house of partnership. A horoscope writer may say that over the next couple of weeks you may be doing some contract negotiations, getting into partnerships, and even getting into some fights as you try to find common ground.

So yes, you have probably been reading your horoscope wrong your whole life... which is why it felt wrong.

On the Cusp

House cusps are boundary lines between houses that show which sign rules which house. House cusps depend on what method of house system you are using. The majority of prediction horoscopes are written using the whole-sign house system, which doesn't take into account the degrees of the planets when making your astrology chart.

However, not all natal charts are calculated with whole-sign houses. One popular system, called the Placidus house system, uses the degrees your rising sign was in the moment you were born to create your chart. A zodiac sign is thirty degrees long, as planets move in degrees from one sign to the next (twelve signs times thirty degrees each equals 360 degrees of the full circle). This makes your chart a little messier. If you have done your natal chart with a generator that uses the Placidus system, you may have noticed some unusual things: the same sign ruling two different houses, missing a sign, or having a planet being in a different house than you thought. This is just how Placidus is calculated. Rest assured, all twelve signs of the zodiac are represented in your chart; they might just not be the ruler of the house.

For this chapter, we will be using the whole-sign houses to determine cusp rulers as it is simpler for first-time astrology witches. However, if you're interested in Placidus, feel free to use that, as neither system is better than the other.

The Houses and Witchcraft

So, what do houses have to do with witchcraft? Well, by learning where the planets are moving in your natal chart, you can learn how to best use the house's power and harness its magical energy. It can also help you learn more about yourself and highlight the unique themes of your life. You may be more attracted to love spells because you have your natal Venus in your pleasure house. You may be a coven leader if Aries rules your community house.

It also helps you find the right timing to do certain spells or make certain decisions simply by where the current planets are moving in your natal houses. For example, let's say you're a Pisces rising, and the sun, moon, and Mercury are all currently in Aquarius. Aquarius rules your twelfth house, the house of the subconscious mind. So, this may be a period of ending, privacy, and self-refection. It would be wise to start meditation, do a tarot spread, or even find unique ways to get grounded during this time as you become more connected with your original magic. Throughout this chapter, we'll be learning more about what the houses represent, what spells are best to cast when the current planets transit into that house, and more. This chapter will not focus on natal houses or what each sign or natal planet means in each house; there are plenty of books that go further in depth about that (see page 168). This chapter will give you a general idea of what houses are and how you can use them. However, keep your natal chart out so you can see which signs rule your own houses and apply them to your life accordingly. For instance, if Leo rules your partnership house (the seventh), you may want to perform the Leo spell found on page 50—but make it about finding partnerships and love.

The 1st House: The Self

Known as the house of the self, the first house is where your rising sign rules. This house represents your appearance, the first impressions you give, your outer behavior, your body, and your overall outlook on life. When planets, especially the sun, transit through your

SPELLS AND RITUALS: Glamour spells, starting new rituals, spells that move your body, getting sigil tattoos, manifesting new opportunities, starting new projects, mantras

first house, it is a period of celebration as you honor yourself. This is a time of new beginnings, changing your appearance, and just putting yourself out there into new situations. Take in all opportunities right now as it is your season to shine.

The 2nd House: Values

Known as the house of values, the second house rules over your material possessions. The sign that rules this house influences how you manage your money, what you put a price on, what you're willing to pay for, how you earn and spend money, and your own self-esteem. When planets transit through the

SPELLS AND RITUALS: Abundance and prosperity spells, marketing your "witchy" services for money, casting attachment spells, manifesting material goods, self-love rituals, self-esteem charms

second house, money becomes deeply important. You are spending money faster than ever, but you get to make it back quickly. It is also a good time to look at your personal resources and what you truly value in your life.

The 3rd House: Communication

Known as the house of communication, the third house rules over how you communicate your thoughts. The sign that rules this house influences how you process information, how you speak and write, how you learn, your type of intelligence, and what you find interesting. When planets transit through the third house, you are often more talkative than usual. You

> **SPELLS AND RITUALS:** Speaking your spells aloud or writing them down, reading books about witchcraft, taking classes about certain parts of witchcraft that interest you, attending coven meetings, travel spells, technology spells, study spells, communicating with spirits

can easily learn new languages, take short classes, or learn things with ease. It's a good time to take a short trip, buy a car or other method of transportation, and visit friends you haven't seen. It is also an ideal time to befriend neighbors or chat with your siblings.

The 4th House: Domestic Life

Known as the house that is really a home, the fourth house represents your domestic and private life. The sign that rules the fourth house influences your relationship with your family, how you were as a child, your traditions, your property, and who you are emotionally. When planets transit your fourth house, you start to think about what makes you feel safe and secure. It's a period of buying

> **SPELLS AND RITUALS:** Placing protection spells and sigils on your home, cleaning your space of negative energy, creating home altars, grounding spells, developing self-care rituals, healing the inner child, creating a solid emotional foundation, visiting family and/or setting boundaries

or renting a house or apartment, connecting with family members and your ancestral roots, resolving issues in your private life, and making things feel secure.

The 5th House: Pleasure

Known as the house of pleasure, the fifth house is where all the fun is at. The sign that rules the fifth house influences how5thyou express yourself, both creatively and romantically, what kind of hobbies you have, how you like to play, your sex drive, and what you enjoy. When planets move into your fifth house, it's all about having fun. This is a time for indulging in new love affairs, relighting the passions in older ones, enjoying your hobbies and leisure time, starting creative projects, and just having a good old time.

> **SPELLS AND RITUALS:** Love spells, glamour magic, romantic rituals, fertility spells, creative ways of expressing magic (making art, writing, performances, etc.), drawing sigils, sex magic, going to concerts and other live events, luck spells, creativity spells

The 6th House: Health

Known as the house of health, the sixth house rules over your vitality and the work you do to take care of yourself and others. The sign that rules the sixth house influences your relationships when it comes to helping and healing, your work ethic, how easy or difficult it is to stick to habits (or break them), and the duties you have to others and yourself. When planets transit through your sixth house, you are encouraged to take a good look at your health and how you can best take care of yourself. You also may take on more responsibilities during this time, start new routines, develop habits; this house can also influence what's going on in your work life.

> **SPELLS AND RITUALS:** Employment spells, healing spells, studying herbalism, kitchen magic, making herbal teas, forming new daily rituals (a daily tarot pull, a morning meditation, visualizing at night, etc.), volunteer work, helping fellow witches, adopting a familiar (or just a pet)

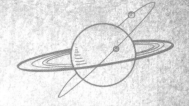

The 7th House: Partnership

Known as the house of partnership, this house deals with relationships of all forms: lovers, spouses, best friends, creative partners, business partners, even your enemies. All your long-term relationships are found here. The sign that rules the seventh house influences who you are when you're in a relationship.

SPELLS AND RITUALS: Binding spells, ethical love spells, attraction spells, looking for your twin flame (cosmic soulmate), signing contracts, handfasting ceremonies, victory spells, teaming up with other witches

It also influences the characteristics of who your "ideal" partner is. When planets transit through your seventh house, it's a period of long-term partnerships, from signing contracts to saying wedding vows. You are looking for partnerships that can help you through this life and become your better self (possibly with your better half). It is also a time of competition and fighting your opponents.

The 8th House: Transformation

Known as the house of transformation, this house deals with all matters of taboo: from sex to death and everything in between. This is also said to be the house of witchcraft as it is the house of the occult. The sign that rules the eighth house represents your witch self. It influences what kind of magic you are drawn to, your skills as a witch, and how your magic flows in general. Apart from magic, it also

SPELLS AND RITUALS: Divination, mediumship, spirit boards, prosperity spells, sex magic, banishing spells, binding spells, cord cutting rituals, transformation magic, celebrating the dead rituals, intimate coven meetings, rebirth rituals, performing rituals sky-clad (naked)

represents the bonds you form in life, how you share wealth, your sexuality, your thoughts on death, and how you move through the phases of life. When planets enter your eighth house, it's usually a period of big changes and transformation, whether you are forming a deeper intimacy with another person, inheriting money, or needing to walk away from something you thought would last forever.

The 9th House: Spirituality

Known as the house of spirituality and expansion, this house represents your spiritual side. The sign that rules over the ninth house influences what you believe in, from your life's philosophy and your personal beliefs to where you place your faith. It also influences what you may study in college and the places and ways you like to travel. When planets transit into your ninth house, you have opportunities for long-distance travel, going to college, having adventures, and discovering something new—either about your culture or the world around you. It is a time of expanding your mind and heart.

> **SPELLS AND RITUALS:** Travel spells, learning new elements of magic, meditation, listening to new perspectives from other witches, law spells, justice rituals, strengthening faith rituals, tarot readings

The 10th House: Public Image

Known as the house of public image, the tenth house rules over your career and ambitions. The sign that rules the tenth house influences the career you have, the reputation you have with the public, the goals you strive to achieve, your ambitions, and your power. It also shows up in the ways you contribute to society and your personal influence. When planets transit through your tenth house, you will be dealing with issues regarding your career, either getting a promotion, making a career change, or looking for a new job. It is also a time to achieve some long-term goals and get recognized for the arduous work you have done.

> **SPELLS AND RITUALS:** Job spell, manifestation, vision boards, prosperity spells, mantras, aura readings, endurance spells, energy spells and brews

The 11th House: Community

Known as the house of community, the eleventh house rules over your social life. The sign that rules over this house influences who you are as a friend and the traits and characteristics of desired friends. This house influences your coven, the things that you wish for, your humanitarian issues, and your dreams. When planets transit through the eleventh house, it's an excellent time to make wishes, make new friends and visit your established friendships, and try to make a difference in your community. It's also a good time to upgrade your electronic devices.

SPELLS AND RITUALS: Techno spells, volunteer work, manifestation, dream magic, making wishes, holding coven meetings, abundance spells, group spells and rituals, spells for new friends, spells to soothe social anxiety, unique rituals, performing good deeds

The 12th House: The Subconscious

Known as the house of the subconscious mind, the twelfth house is where all your secrets are kept–even the ones you don't know about. The sign that rules over the twelfth house influences your need for privacy, the way you handle secrets, your fears, the dreams you have, your hidden talents, and how you both hurt and heal yourself. When planets transit through your twelfth house, it's a time of endings, and how you handle them influences the next phase. It's also a time of sacrifices as you need to let go of things to move forward. It could be healing, or it could lead to your undoing. Whatever the case will be, you'll need time alone to unravel your inner mysteries.

SPELLS AND RITUALS: Healing spells, dream magic, aura cleansing, cord cutting rituals, karmic returns, journaling, meditation, hypnosis, truth-telling spells, sleeping brews, divination, private practice

Your Cosmic Journey

While we have reached the end of this book, we have only just scratched the surface on the fascinating and extensive subject of astrology. This book gives you the basic language of the cosmos; it's now up to you to use that language to piece together what it means for your life and your magic journey—even if it is just understanding what a retrograde is or that you're more than just your sun sign.

Now it is your turn to go off and use your knowledge of the heavenly bodies to add to your craft, from performing rituals on the new moon to casting bold and fiery spells when Mercury is in Leo. In life and in magic, timing is everything, and I hope you use the magic of astrology to make the most of its energy.

But more than anything, I hope you have a stronger sense of connection between you, the sky, and the endless source of magic that flows between. I hope you stand before a full moon and be in awe of her powers. I hope you see all the stars in the night sky and remember that you are also made up of magic yourself.

Remember, this is only the beginning.